AF657877

FORENSIC INSECT SCIENCE

FORENSIC INSECT SCIENCE

By

Dr. T.V. Sathe
Department of Zoology
Shivaji University
Kolhapur - 416 004
(Maharashtra)
(INDIA)

&

Dr. Divya K. Jadav
Department of Zoology
Shivaji University
Kolhapur - 416 004
(Maharashtra)
(INDIA)

D P H

DISCOVERY PUBLISHING HOUSE PVT. LTD.
INDIA

Published by:

Namit Wasan

DISCOVERY PUBLISHING HOUSE PVT. LTD.

4383/4B, Ansari Road, Darya Ganj
New Delhi-110 002 (India)
Phone : +91-11-23279245, 43596064-65
Fax : +91-11-23253475
E-mail : discoverypublishinghouse@gmail.com
namitwasan9@gmail.com
sales@discoverypublishinggroup.com

website: www.discoverypublishinggroup.com

First Edition: **2017**

ISBN: 978-93-5056-841-5

Forensic Insect Science

© **Authors**

All rights reserved. No part of this publication should be reproduced, stored in a retrieval system, or transmitted in any form or by any means: electronic, mechanical, photocopying, recording or otherwise, without the prior written permission of the author and the publisher.

This book has been published in good faith that the material provided by authors is original. Every effort is made to ensure accuracy of material, but the editor, publisher and printer will not be held responsible for any inadvertent error(s). In case of any dispute, all legal matters are to be settled under Delhi jurisdiction only.

Printed at:
Infinity Imaging Systems
Delhi

PREFACE

Forensic entomology deals with the use of insect evidences in courts of law. Forensic insects help in solving the problems related to murder, suicide, rape, physical abuse and contraband trafficking. Two major groups of insects that are attracted to carcass and provide valuable information in forensic investigation are the dipterous flies and the coleopterous beetles. Several other insects can also play an important role in solving forensic problems. Therefore, studying the diversity, biology, ecology and making the index of forensic insects of a region is essential part of forensic science. The developmental factors of forensic insects tell us the exact time of death of a person. Insects also tell us the route used by culprit in certain forensic cases, the toxicity caused in the case and the environment of forensic events. The carcasses undergo five stages of decomposition. At each stage of decomposition particular group of insects is associated. In the first stage, especially blowflies and flesh flies are attracted. The adults and maggots of blowflies and flesh flies are most widely used in the investigation. At the latter stages of decomposition beetles dominant the scene. Apart from the use of insects in estimating PMI they have their own economic value. Blowflies and flesh flies cause myiasis in human and livestock. The maggots appeared to possess exceptional healing properties and clinical trials on the treatment of chronic osteomyelitis. Blowflies play a valuable role as pollinators. The knowledge of diversity, biology and ecology of forensic insects occurring on the carrion under prevailing local environmental conditions, provides investigators with valuable data to solve legal cases. Therefore, the present work has tremendous importance in forensic scene. We feel that this work will be stimulatory and attractive to the students, teachers and scientists working in the field of forensic science and life science.

Dr. T.V. Sathe

Dr. Divya Jadav. K

CONTENTS

1 INTRODUCTION

Among the other planets in solar system Earth is unique in many ways. One of its reason is it sustain life forms. The geographical area of India (Fig.1.1) is about 329 million hectares and its coastline stretches to nearly 7000 km., (Jairajpuri, 1991). Zoogeographically, India belongs to oriental realm, with rich biodiversity, however, the Ethiopian, Palearctic species and some belonging to other realms are also found in India. Insects have roamed the earth for 250 million years (Castner, 2004). Presently, there are about 700,000 described species. According to Starkeby (2004) there may be more than 10 million species of insects on the earth.

Maharashtra (Fig. 1.2) is one of the leading states in India in biodiversity, agriculture and industrialization which occupies the western and central part of the country and has a long coastline stretching nearly 720 km along the Arabian Sea (Anonymous, 2014). One of the more prominent physical features of Maharashtra is the Deccan plateau, which is separated from the Konkan coastline by 'Ghats' (Anonymous, 2012). The state is surrounded by Gujarat to the north west, Madhya Pradesh to the north, Chhattisgarh to the east, Telangana to the south east, Karnataka to the south and Goa to the south west (Anonymous, 2014). The Western Ghats better known as Sahyadri, are a hilly range running parallel to the coast, at an average elevation of 1,200 meters (4,000 ft) (Anonymous, 2014). The main rivers of the state are: Krishna, Bhima, Godavari, Tapi-Purna and Wardha-Wainganga (Anonymous, 2014). The Flora of Maharashtra is heterogeneous in composition. In 2012 the recorded thick forest area in the state was 61,939 km^2 which was about 20.13 per cent of the state's geographical area (WCTMGM, 2014).

Biodiversity plays an important role in sustainable development of a country or a region. Western Ghats is biodiversity rich area of India and among 35 hot spots of the world. It is under serious threat due to human interference in forest ecosystems. Western Ghats of Maharashtra is located between 8°20′-20° 40′ N latitude and 73°-77° E longitude at an average elevation of 3900ft with about 2000-6000 mm rainfall (Anonymous, 2014).

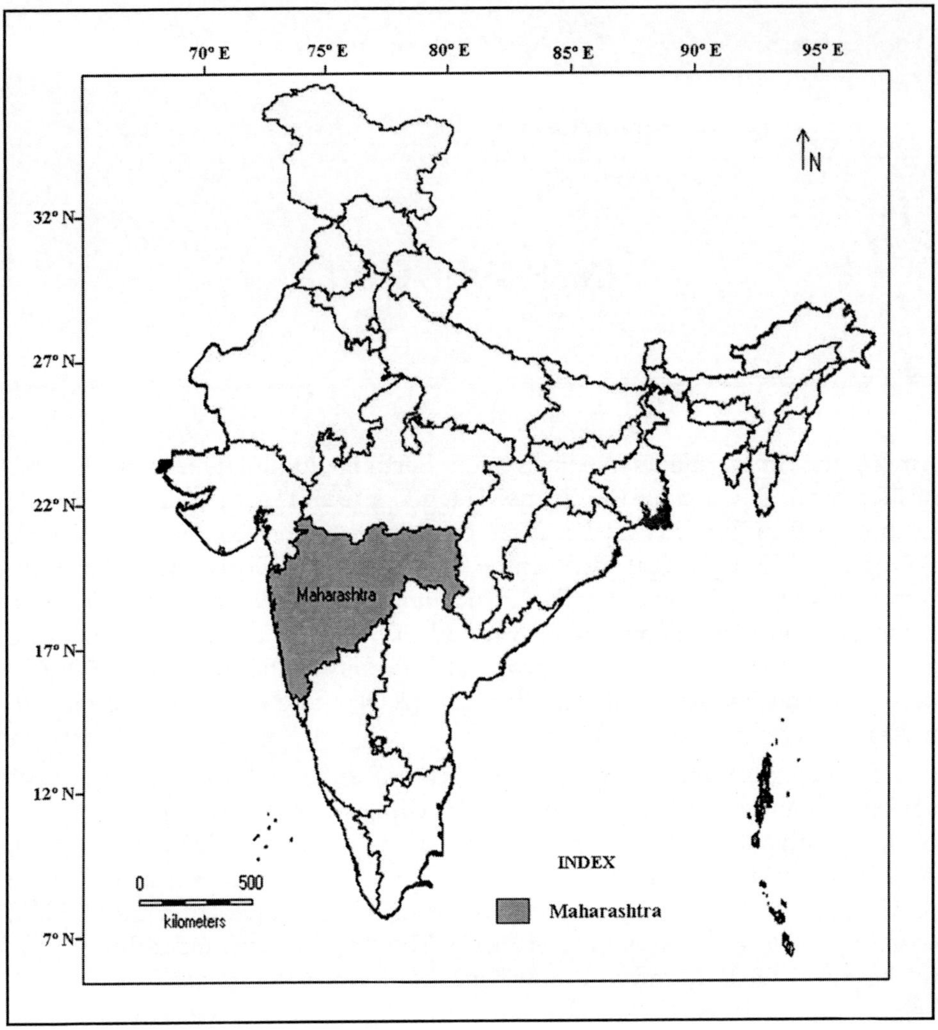

Fig. 1.1: **Map of India Showing Maharashta**

Kolhapur district (Fig.1.3) in Maharashtra, is leading district in agriculture and forestry which is the southernmost district of Maharashtra and is one of the industrially developed district. Kolhapur is an ancient city situated on the bank of river Panchaganga and is known as 'Dakshin Kashi'.

The district of Kolhapur lies in the south-west of Maharashtra between 15° to 17° N latitude and 73° to 74° E longitude and spreads across the Deccan Platue in the rain shadow region of the Sahyadri mountain, ranges on the southernmost tip of the state of Maharashtra. The Sangli district lies to the north, the Belgaum district of Karnataka State is to the east and south, Ratnangiri and Sindhudurg districts of Maharashtra are to the West. To the west, the Sahyadri ranges are located and the river Warana is to the north

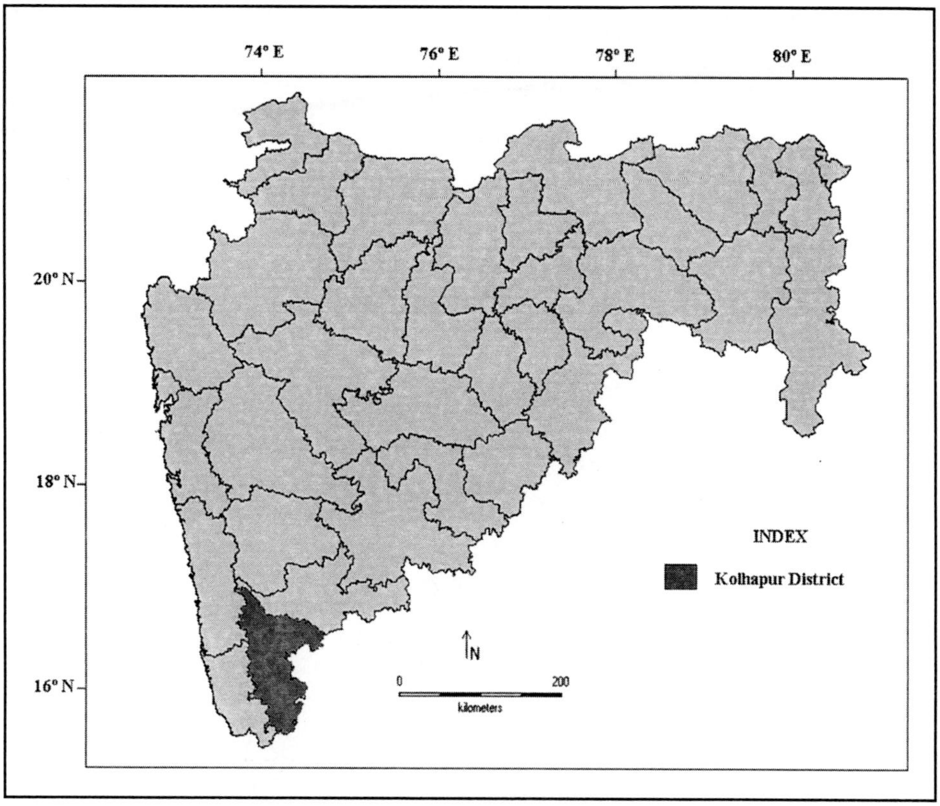

Fig. 1.2: **Map of Maharashta Showing Kolhapur District**

which forms the natural boundaries to the district. It has an area of 7685.00 sq.km., which is about 2.5 per cent of total area of the state and it ranks 24th in the state as far as area is concerned.

The climate of the Kolhapur plain is temperate and similar to the other districts of Bombay Deccan adjoining the Ghats. In the western part of Kolhapur near the Sahyadris, it is always cooler than that in the eastern part which is liable to hot winds during April and May. The nights over the whole district are generally cool due to the influence of the sea breezes which set in during the afternoons and continue till late in the evening. The whole year climate of Kolhapur district may be divided into three periods namely: *(i)* hot weather period from March to May, *(ii)* rainy period from June to October and *(iii)* cold weather period from November to February.

The district receives rain from the South-West as well as North-East monsoons. The proportion of rainfall decreases very sharply from the west to east ranging between the maximum of 6000 mm in the west to the minimum of 600 mm in the east. The physical setting of the Kolhapur district is divided into three main parts: Eastern ranges, Central ranges and Southern ranges.

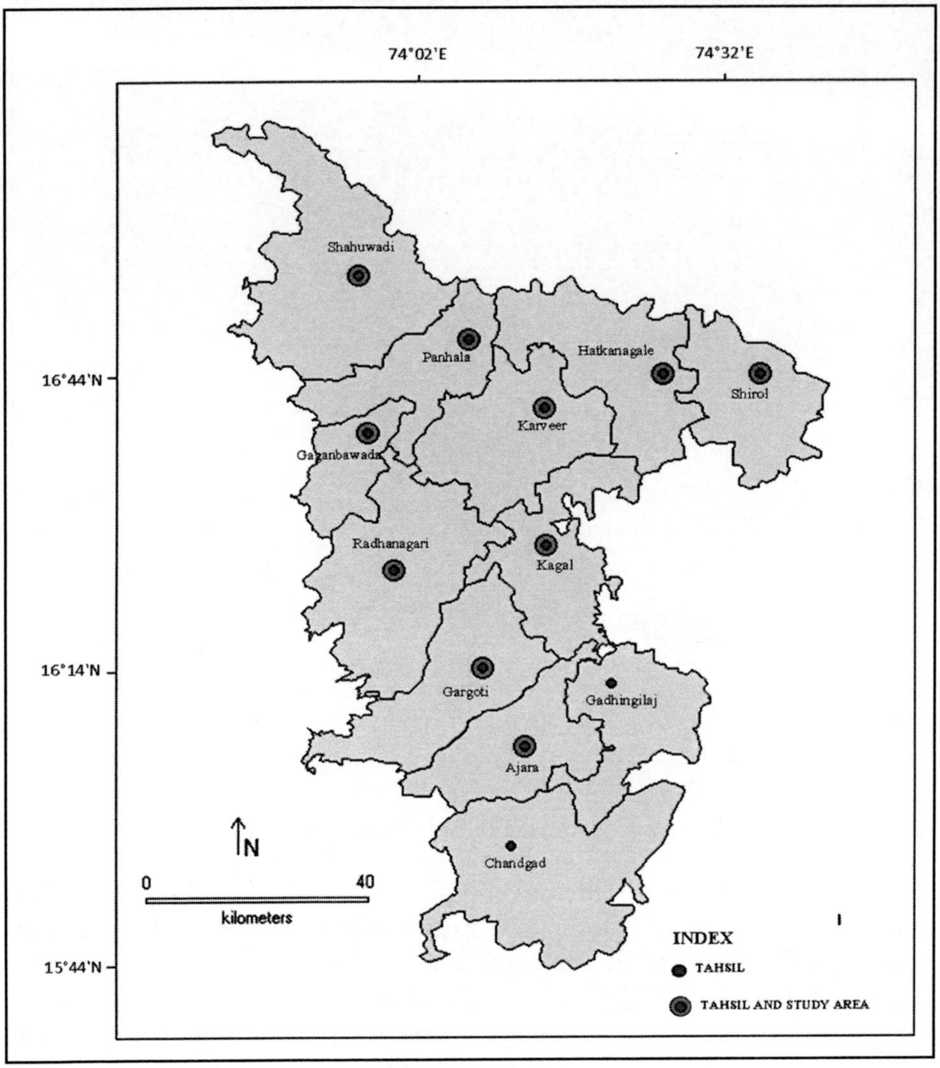

Fig. 1.3: **Map of Kolhapur District (Study Area)**

Eastern and Central ranges have black soil formed from lava, and at some places it has large tracts of fertile land. The western ranges are mostly hilly and have red soil. The majority area in the west is under thick forest coverage (http://shodhganga.inflibnet.ac.in/bitstream/10603/4312/8/08). The population of Kolhapur city is 3,876,001 with sex ratio male: female (1:0.958) (1,980,658:1,895,343) (http://www.census2011.co.in/census/district/368-kolhapur.html). Occupationally population comprised as farmers, industry workers, labours, students, teachers, officers and several other kinds due to their different types of duties and there by forensic problems too.

Forensic entomology, in the broad sense, is the term applied to the use of entomological (insects) evidences in courts of law (Haskell, 2006). It is a multi-disciplinary field which implies Taxonomy, Ecology, Biology and Toxicology. The urban entomology, involves the study of insects which affect the human environment, such as: structural damage by termites, carpenter ants and even spider bites (Haskell *et al.* 1997; Sathe, 2013) and stored products entomology involves the studies of insects and insect residues in stored products such as: grain and flour (Anderson, 2001). According to Anderson (2001) the study of medicolegal or medicocriminal aspects of insects is termed as 'forensic entomology'. The medico-legal aspects of forensic entomology includes involvement of insects and other arthropod in events such as: murder, suicide and rape but also includes physical abuse and contraband trafficking (Cruz, 2006).

The first forensic entomology case is reported by Chinese lawyer and death investigator Sung TŸu in the 13th century in the medico - legal text book, His yûan chi lu (one possible translation: washing away of wrongs) (Benecke, 2001). The classic work in the field of forensic entomology enabled identifications of many insects (Mégnin, 1887,1894). Many medical professionals and pathologists were interested in entomology in France (Bergeret, 1855; Megnin, 1894) and Canada (Johnston and Villeneuve, 1897). In India, the earliest study on this subject is believed to be by Mackenzie in Calcutta (Indian Medical Gazette, 1889; 167) where he made observations on dead bodies about the time of appearance of eggs and maggots (Modi, 1999).

The forensic insect diversity varies with different eco-systems depending on the habitat of the carrion as well as that of buried and unburied cadavers. Such difference in diversity paves way for possible suspicion/prediction about any crime (Varatharajan and Sen, 2000).

According to Anderson and Cervenka (2007) one such habitat, providing an excellent food source for a more or less specialized insect community, is a vertebrate corpse.

The breakdown of organic substances into simpler forms is the process of decomposition. Decomposing bodies of carcasses undergo biological, chemical and physical changes and at each stage of decomposition, they are invaded by a specific species of insects, often in a predictable sequence (Van *et al.* 1999). These changes are depends on interrelated factors such as: climate, situation and insect access (Turner, 1991). In the decomposition process the microorganisms, insects and vertebrates such as: birds and mammals plays a vital role. There are five general stages used to describe the process of decomposition in vertebrate animals' *viz;* Fresh, Bloat, Active and Advanced Decay, and Dry/Remains (Payne, 1965). According to Carter *et al.* (2007) the fresh stage begins immediately after the heart stops beating. During this stage the cadaver undergoes various process of decomposition such as: rigor mortis, algor mortis, autolysis and putrefaction. The accumulation of gases within the bodily cavity causes the distention of abdomen and gives a cadaver its overall bloated appearance (Carter *et al.* 2008). The pressure combined with the loss of integrity of the skin causes the body to rupture (Carter *et al.* 2008). During the active decay period greatest mass loss is due to both the voracious feeding of maggots and the purging of decomposition fluids into the surrounding environment (Carter *et al.* 2008).

Carter *et al.* (2008) says that decomposition is largely inhibited during advanced decay due to the loss of readily available cadaveric material which leads to change in pH and a significant increase in soil nitrogen (Vass *et al.* 1992). According to Bhawara *et al.* (2008) there are two main ways by which insects can be used to determine elapsed time since death are:

- *Entomological succession*: useful when the corpse has been dead for between a month up to a year or more.
- *Maggot's age and development*: useful when the corpse has been dead less than a month prior to discovery.

Apart from estimating PMI, there are several other types of information that can be derived from insects found at a crime scene (Benecke, 1998, 2004) such as:

- Suspects have been linked to a scene of crime as a result of the fact that they had been bitten by arthropods specific to the vicinity (Prichard *et al.* 1986; Webb *et al.* 1983).
- Insects that live in restricted areas but are found on a corpse in a different area can prove that the body had been moved after death.
- Blowfly larvae can give information on how long children or elderly people were neglected by their relatives or nursing personnel.
- Aspects of hygiene (*e.g.*, appearance of larvae and flies in clean, empty rooms, or of maggots in food) can be explained by linking the entomological findings to known death cases or other environmental factors from the surrounding to known death cases or other environmental factors from the surroundings of the death scene.
- Drugs that cannot be detected in severely decomposed tissue of a corpse may still be found in the insects that did feed on the corpse.
- The location of a stab wound can be determined by unusual feeding sites of beetles and maggots (Merkel, 1925).
- The question of whether a person was killed and brought outside during day or night time while it was raining or not may be scrutinized (Benecke, 2001; Nuorteva, 1977; Benecke, 1996; Schroeder *et al.* 2002; Lord, 1990).

Smith (1986) says that, four categories of insects can be found on decomposing carrion: *(i)* Necrophagous species feeding on the carrion; *(ii)* Predators and parasites feeding on the necrophagous species: this group also contains schizophagous species which feed on the body first and which become predaceous on the later stages; *(iii)* Omnivorous species feeding on the carrion and other arthropods like: ants, wasps and some beetles; *(iv)* Other species like: springtails and spiders which use the corpse as an extension of their environment.

Insects mostly involved in the forensic investigations are true flies of order Diptera (Joseph *et al.* 2011). About 150,000 species belonging to 158 families have been identified and de-scribed as forensic insects. Out of which 285 species come from the family Fanniidae, 5,000 from the family Muscidae, 1,500 from the family Caliphoridae and 2,500 species from the family Sarcophagidae (Carvalho *et al.* 2003; Goddard, 2007; Carvalho and Patiu, 2008). Forensic flies are very fast and can mechanically and non-mechanically transmit numerous pathogens to human's food and living environment especially in warm seasons (Service, 2008; Goddard, 2007). In addition, their larvae can contaminate human and animal tissues and organs and cause myiasis (Service, 2008; Shayeghi *et al.* 2011). Myiasis is the infestation of tissues of live vertebrates (human and/or animals) by dipterous larvae (Kuria *et al.* 2010). Blow flies such as: *Chrysomya albiceps* (Wiedemann) and *Lucilia sericata* (Meigen) (Diptera: Calliphoridae) and flesh flies such as: *Sarcophaga spp.* (Diptera: Sarcophagidae) are widely distributed throughout the world and characterized as a facultative ectoparasites responsible for primary or secondary myiasis in humans and livestock (Zumpt, 1965; Smith, 1986; Hall and Wall, 1995; Anderson, 2000; Grassberger *et al.* 2003).

Coleopteran families namely Histeridae, Staphylinidae, Silphidae, Cleridae, Dermestidae and Tenebrionidae have the tremendous forensic value since they predominate the scene (Reed, 1958; Payne, 1965; Braack, 1986; Goff *et al.* 1986; Goff, 1993; Tantawi *et al.* 1996). The coleopterans have the fore-wings hardened into elyptra or wing cases, which usually cover the abdomen, giving the insect an armour- plated appearance. They are tough insects of size ranging from 0.5mm to 150mm in length. The Coleoptera is the largest order of insects with over 275000 known species. Some forensically important beetle families are: Carabidae, Silphidae, Staphylinidae, Histeridae, Cleridae, Dermestidae, Trogidae, Scarabaeidae, etc. Morley (1907) over a period of ten years, found 113 speies, of which he regarded 37 as genuine flesh eaters.

The parasitic order Hymenoptera is also relevantly used in forensic entomology to evaluate the time of death. Hymenoptera parasitoids of the larvae and pupae of flies may play an important role in the estimation of the post-mortem period because their time of attack is often restricted to a small, well-defined window of time in the development of the host insect (Frederickx *et al.* 2013). The families namely Braconidae, Pteromalidae, Encyrtidae, Diapriidae and Figitidae are mostly involved in forensic science (Frederickx *et al.* 2013). According to Rocha *et al.* (2009), to establish a reliable forensic entomological framework, it is necessary the basic knowledge of biological and ecological aspects of their species in a particular space and time.

The temperature of the crime scene is very important factor and it rarely happens that the criminal is thoughtful enough to kill their victim right underneath the weather station (Bhawara *et al.* 2008). The results from the forensic entomologist are not immediate as it takes time to rear immature stages. This is possible in situation of freezing, deep buried and wrapped bodies. Insect succession differs from geographic region and species and time of arrival of insects also vary accordingly (Bhawara *et al.* 2008).

A thorough knowledge of life cycle duration, age and stage of the insect occurring on the carrion along with data on other cohabiting insect species, under prevailing local environmental conditions, provides investigators with valuable data to form a template for dating the remains (Bhawara *et al.* 2008). Kolhapur region of India is recognised as biodiversity rich area since some part of Western Ghats is located in the same district which is among the 35 hot spots of the world for biodiversity, conservation and protection. Periodic surveys and resurveys of forensic insects are important part of forensic science for understanding the occurrence and availability of forensic insects.

Hence, the present study is objected for diversity, biology and ecology of forensically important blowflies, flesh flies, beetles and other insects. The present work will be helpful for exploiting the forensic fauna in medico legal practices in near future.

2 REVIEW OF LITERATURE

INTERNATIONAL

Review of literature indicated that, sizable work is reported in forensic entomology at global scenario. Notable work in forensic entomology is given below. Early historical account of forensic insects is almost non-existent. However, Chinese first reported case of a man dying of wounds inflicted by sickle which was detected with the help of insects in 13th century. Later Europeans used insects in forensic cases (Sathe *et al.* 2013).

According to Bergeret (1855) first application of forensic entomology in a French courtroom was in 1850, can be viewed as a breakthrough for this discipline. Skeletonized remains of a child were found behind a chimney by workmen during redecoration. This insect evidence was accepted as proof for the first time for solving the mystery of murder. At that time, forensic examiners had only a poor understanding of insect biology and their knowledge was based largely on casual observations.

Yovanovich (1888) and Megnin (1894) were the first forensic examiners who attempted to evaluate insect succession on corpses. Their work was found for establishing the science of forensic entomology properly. Johnston and Villeneuve (1897), Leclercq and Leclercq (1948), Nuorteva (1959a, 1959b), Leclercq (1968, 1969, 1983, 1997), and Nuorteva *et al.* (1974) were among the first to use forensic entomology for the determination of the minimum post mortem interval.

Many others like Marchenko (1980, 1988, 2001), Erzinclioglu (1983, 1986, 1986, 2003), Rodriguez and Bass (1983), Greenberg (1985), Nishida *et al.* (1986), Lord *et al.* (1986), Turner (1987), Goff *et al.* (1989) and Goff (1991) have laid stress on the importance of insect evidence during forensic investigations.

Review of literature reveals that very little is known on the survey and surveillance of forensic insects. Simmons (1925) studied the life cycle of the Ham beetle, *Necrobia rufipes* (DeGeer) and reported that, the adult may live for more than 14 months, the female depositing as many as 2,100 eggs during its survival period. In warm weather the incubation period was four days or more. The preoviposition period was as brief as two days. The period from hatching of the egg to adult emergence was as short as 30 days, including 17 days as growing larva and 13 days within the cocoon.

Knipling (1939) determined larvae implicated in infestations in wounds and cases of cutaneous myiasis in the United States. Pessôa and Lane (1941) studied Scarabaeinae fauna of legal medicine interest, found in São Paulo and neighborhood Brazil comprising 113 species of 26 genera. One of the important studies on insects and their relationship to decay rates was undertaken by Reed (1958) on 45 dog carcasses which revealed much information on the ecological process and stages of decomposition. It was reported that the total arthropod populations were greater in summer; however, certain species reached their maximum population during the cooler periods of the year.

Burger (1965) studied the succession of sarcophagous Diptera in different seasons of the year on mammalian carcasses. According to Payne (1965) a definite ecological succession occurred among the fauna of carrion. Each stage of decay was characterized by a particular group of arthropods or insects each of which occupied a particular niche. Nuorteva (1966) studied the flying activity of *Phormia terraenovae* Robineau-Desvoidy in subarctic conditions. During the studies he trapped 10604 flies out of which 8737 belonging to the species *P. terraenovae.*

Kurahashi (1971) studied Australian and oriental Calliphora under 5 genera and reported that genus Calliphora has a number of members with greater diversity of form and coloration. Lane (1975) studied the blow fly succession on white mice, so as to calculate precisely and accurately the time of death within a period of 4 to 5 days after death during which blow flies were the most significant insects present.

Denno and Cothran (1976) studied the competitive interactions and ecological strategies of Sarcophagid and Calliphorid flies inhabiting rabbit carrion. Hanski (1976) carried out two breeding experiments in Southern Finland with the community of fly larvae living in carrion. Hanski (1977) reported 4 species of calliphorids in Canary Islands during last 150 years. He also studied their biogeography and ecology of flies. Kurahashi (1981) studied 12 species of Calliphorid flies from Fiji and keyed and treated including 8 species previously known from Fiji and described 3 new species of the genus *Onesia* (Diptera: Calliphoridae).

O'Flynn (1983a) added notes on the biology of *Chrysomya nigripes* Aubertin, an important component of the carrion fauna of southeastern Queensland. It appears to prefer carrion in a more advanced state of decomposition than other species of *Chrysomya* in the area. O'Flynn (1983b) reported the succession and rate of development of insects in carrion is potentially a useful and accurate tool for determining the length of time elapsed since death. Mazur (1984) published a world catalog of Histeridae in which 332 genera, 75 subgenera 3793 species and 48 subspecies of family Histeridae.

Erzinclioglu (1985) provided descriptions based on a dctailed comparative study of the structural features of all three larval instars and pupae of the six British *Calliphora* and single *Chrysomya* species. Results demonstrated that certain characters, singly or in combination, enable reliable species separation and keys were provided to third instar larvae and pupae of all these species. Dear (1985) provided the key to the Fauna of New Zealand's Calliphoridae. Keys are also given to genera and species with diagnostic characters and systematic importance of the 7 genera including 54 species. He also gave checklist for subfamily Calliphorinae.

Smith (1986) described the faunal succession on dead bodies that included exposed, buried, mummified, and burnt bodies. He also discussed how the environmental conditions like temperature, humidity and light influence the fauna on the body. Chen (1987) studied the responses of nondiapausing flesh fly *Sarcophaga crassipalpis* Macquart (Diptera: Sarchophagidae) to low rearing temperature. Rearing temperature greatly influence cold tolerance pharate adults reared at 15°C.

Holloway (1991) studied the morphological characters to identify adult *Lucillia cuprina* (Wiedemann) and *Lucillia sericata* (Meign). Isiche *et al.* (1992) found a difference in the Calliphorid species abundance and diversity on mouse carrion in sunny and shaded habitats. El-Kady *et al.* (1994) carried out field studies on blow fly and flesh fly succession on exposed rabbit carcasses killed by different causes. They noted that decomposition of carcasses varied according to the manner of killing. Tantawi *et al.* (1996) studied arthropod succession on exposed rabbit carcasses in Egypt.

Queiroz (1996) studied the life cycle of *Chrysomya albiceps* (Wiedmann) at different temperatures. The basal temperatures for the larval and pupal stage and for the larval and adult phase were 15.04, 17.39 and 15.38°C. Queiroz *et al.* (1997) studied morphological aspects of the larval instars of *C. albiceps* (Diptera, Calliphoridae). Tomberlin and Adler (1998) made a comparative study on seasonal colonization and decomposition pattern of rat carrion in water and on land in an open field. Saunders *et al.* (1999) studied the survival and reproduction of small blowflies *Calliphora vicina* Robineau-Desvoidy produced in severely overcrowded short day larval cultures.

Carvalho *et al.* (2000) prepared checklist of arthropods associated with pig carrion and human corpses in Southeastern Brazil of 36 families of insects including- Calliphoridae, Sarcophagidae, Muscidae (Diptera) and Dermestidae (Coleoptera). Ma (2000) studied constitution and succession of insect community on pig carcass in Hangzhou. Sukontason *et al.* (2003a) made a survey of forensically-relevant fly species in Chiang Mai, northern Thailand.

Survey was carried out at six mountain sites representing different areas around downtown Chiang Mai and collected a total of 2,754 flies representing at least 12 genera in 4 families of Diptera.

Sukontason *et al.* (2003b) studied ultrastructure of all larval instars of *Parasarcophaga dux* (Thomson), a common flesh fly species in Thailand. Special attention is given to the structure of anterior and posterior spiracles since these are important features used to differentiate between other sarcophagids. Uiyshen and Hanula (2003) studied the diversity and seasonal activity of carrion beetles (Coleoptera: Silphidae) in Northeastern Georgia. They collected 8 species of silphids.

Chehlarov (2004) reported 59 species belonging to 26 genera from Bulgaria, Greece, Turkey, Slovakia and Macedonia. Five species and 2 genera were new for the Bulgaria. He also provided distributional data for 32 species. Sukontason *et al.* (2005) also studied the morphology of the second and third instars of *Chrysomya villeneuvi* Patton, by use of light microscopy. Both instars were of hairy appearance, bearing elongated tubercles along the abdominal and caudal segments. Kaczorowska (2006) studied Calliphorid species in seventeen localities representing marine habitats and coastal brackish areas, 21 species of these flies were collected, accounting for 31.82 per cent of the Polish fauna of Calliphoridae. Among them, 19 species were new to these habitats.

Martinez *et al.* (2007) was the first to look at insect succession on decomposing carcasses in the high altitude plains (Paramo) in Colombia, at 3035 m above sea level. Five stages of decomposition were designated with indicator species for each stage. Hayat *et al.* (2008) reported a total of 13 species of Sarcophagidae (Diptera) belonging to 2 subfamilies from different localities in Turkey during the years 1994 and 2006. *Wohlfahrtia meigeni* (Schiner, 1862) is recorded for the first time from Turkey. From Turkey 86 species of flesh flies have been reported with new locality recorded 13 species. Khoobdel *et al.* (2008) studied the fauna of Sarcophagidae and Caliphoridae in Tehran and Suburb, during the years 1996-1997 and 2000-02. They identified 22 species of flies. 13 species were medically important and four species consisting; *Calliphora vomitoria* (Linnaeus), *Lucillia richardsi* Collin, *Sarcophaga fertoni* Villeneuve and *Sarcophaga peregrina* Robineau-Desvoidy have been identified and reported for the first time from Iran.

Sukontason *et al.* (2008) again studied the morphology of the egg, larvae, and puparium of *H. ligurriens* Wiedeman a blow fly species of forensic importance in Thailand using scanning electron microscopy (SEM). Almeida and Mise (2009) provided the list of forensic insects of South America comprising 221 species from 15 families, of which 70 per cent of the species were from Brazil. They reported Scarabaeidae as the most diverse family with 121 species, followed by Staphylinidae with 68. They also provided diagnostic key for the families and species.

Tüzün *et al.* (2010) reported a total of 3179 forensic insects belonging to 5 orders (Diptra, Coleoptera, Hymenoptera, Dermaptera and Blattaria), 11 families, 16 genera and 18 species, during the period of 53 days. Morales and Wolff (2010) carried out the city survey of Medellin, Colombia. A total of 11,732 forensic insects were determined, belonging to the classes Insecta and Arachnida. Out of which Diptera corresponding to 98.5 per cent of the total, was the most abundant and diverse group, with 16 families (Calliphoridae, Drosophilidae, Psychodidae, Fanniidae, Muscidae, Milichiidae, Ulidiidae, Scatopsidae, Sepsidae, Sphaeroceridae, Heleomyzidae, Stratiomyidae, Syrphidae, Phoridae, Tephritidae and Curtonotidae) followed by Coleoptera with five families (Carabidae, Staphylinidae, Ptiliidae, Hydrophilidae and Phalacaridae).

Sousa *et al.* (2011) studied diversity of Calliphoridae and Sarcophagidae (Diptera: Oestroidea) in continuous forest and gaps at different stages of regeneration in the Urucu oilfield in western Brazilian Amazonia. Rùžička and Schneider (2011) made taxonomic revision of the subgenus *Deutosilpha* Portevin (of *Necrophila* Kirby and Spence) through southeastern Asia. Dupont *et al.* (2011) studied the carcasses of rats (*Rattus norvegicus* Berkenhout, 1769 var WISTAR) for colonization by the local fauna of arthropods.

Castro *et al.* (2012) reported the occurrence and abundance of the specific groups of Diptera collected on carcasses. In general, the bloated stage recorded higher abundance and species-richness values. Seventy-one species were identified, belonging to 39 families, in a total of 20 144 adult Diptera collected. Bunchu (2012) studied 93 blow fly species belonging to 9 subfamilies, namely: Subfamily Ameniinae, Calliphoridae, Luciliinae, Phumosiinae, Polleniinae, Bengaliinae, Auchmeromyiinae, Chrysomyinae and Rhiniinae.

Bunchu *et al.* (2012) determined the morphology of all stages and the developmental rate of *H. ligurriens* reared under natural ambient conditions in Phitsanulok province, northern Thailand. Kumara *et al.* (2012) surveyed flies attracted to human remains during death investigations in north Peninsular Malaysia. Six families, 8 genera, and 16 species were identified from human remains, with the greatest diversity occurring on remains recovered indoors. A total relative frequency of species was led by *Chrysomya megacephala* (Fabricius) (46%), followed by *C. ruifacies* (Macquart) (22%) and *Sarcophaga* (Liopygia) *ruicornis* (Fabricius) (5%).

Azmi and Lim (2013) determined the dipteran species diversity and their succession over the decomposition period of the rabbit carrions. A total of 229 individuals belonging to 11 species from six families of Diptera were identified in October and December 2007. Dekeirsschieter *et al.* (2013) monitored the presence of adult rove beetles (Coleoptera, Staphylinidae) on decaying pig carcasses in a forest biotope during four seasons (spring, summer, fall, and winter). A total of 23 genera comprising 60 species of rove beetles were collected from pig carcasses. The staphylinid subfamilies identified on pig carcasses were Aleocharinae (13 species), Omaliinae (3 species), Oxytelinae (2 species), Paederinae (1 species), Staphylininae (37 species), and Tachyporinae (8 species). The seasonal species richness was represented by 26 species in summer, 29 species in fall, 32 species in winter, and 36 species in spring.

Aballay *et al.* (2013) presented key to 16 histerid species associated with decaying carcasses in Argentina including diagnoses and habitus photographs for these species. Asenjo *et al.* (2013) provided a complete checklist with new records and geographical distribution of the rove beetles (Coleoptera, Staphylinidae) of Brazil In total, 453 genera and 2,688 species were listed. The staphylinid fauna of Brazil represents approximately 37 per cent of the known fauna in the Neotropical region and 5 per cent of the world. Bousquet *et al.* (2013) made the survey of beetles and provided a checklist of beetles (Coleoptera) of Canada and Alaska presenting in all 8237 species.

Kosmann *et al.* (2013) listed 91 species of 29 genera of Calliphoridae found in the Americas south of Mexico. These species were seven subfamilies of Calliphorinae. Szpila and Pape (2013) studied the morphology of the first instar larva of two species of the genus *Taxigramma* Perris, *T. albina* (Rohdendorf) and *T. karakulensis* (Enderlein).

Pohjoismäki *et al.* (2014) updated checklist of the superfamilies Oestroidea and Hippoboscoidea recorded from Finland. The checklist covers the following families: Calliphoridae, Rhiniidae, Sarcophagidae, Rhinophoridae, Tachinidae, Oestridae and Hippoboscidae. From Calliphoridae 102 species were reported from Europe and 45 from Finland while Family Sarcophagidae was represented by 12 from Europe and 1 from Finland. Fratczak and Matuszewski (2014) taken the measurements which are useful for instar determination of *Necrodes littoralis* (Silphidae) and *Creophilus maxillosus* (Linnaeus) (Staphylinidae) and how to combine them to get accurate and easy to use instar classifier. They measured morphological features.

Yang *et al.* (2014) collected 16 species of Taiwanese calliphorids. They provided dichotomous keys to all subfamilies, tribes, genera and species of blow flies recorded in Taiwan. Shin *et al.* (2015) surveyed 1398 individual samples belonging to 3 orders, 13 families, 18 genera, and 32 species, the dominant family and species were Calliphoridae and *Lucilia sericata* (Meigen) respectively. Augul *et al.* (2015) registered Hairy Rove Beetle, *C. maxillosus* as a new record of Iraqi fauna, which collected from exposed rat carcass *Rattus norvegicus* in decay stage, these specimens had been found feeding on the larvae of *C. albiceps* (Diptera; Calliphoridae). Klimaszewski *et al.* (2015) reported 54 new Canadian provincial aleocharine beetles (Staphylinidae), including three new Canadian records and one new North American record. Roe and Higley (2015) conducted a series of experiments with *Lucilia sericata*, a forensically important blow fly species, that met the requirements needed to create statistically valid development models. Experiments were conducted over 11 temperatures (7.5 to 32.5°C) with a 16:8 L:D cycle.

Sukchit *et al.* (2015) observed insect succession pattern broadly conformed to those reported from other (mostly temperate) regions. The primary and dominant necrophagous colonizers were the Calliphorid dipterans, *C. megacephala* and *Achoetandrus rufifacies* (Macquart), in both habitats. 51 taxa were recorded (33 species, 4 morph species and 14 unidentified beyond order).

National

National review of literature indicates that forensic insects are not so widely used in Indian court of law (Sathe *et al.* 2013; Jadav and Sathe, 2015). Senior-White *et al.* (1940) classified the family Calliphoridae into four subfamilies: Calliphorinae, Chrysomyinae, Rhiniinae and Sarcophaginae and accommodated 214 species from British India under 37 genera. Several Indian workers added on biology and bionomics of the forensic insects. Subramanian and Mohan (1980) studied the life history; bionomics and reproduction strategy of blow flies *C. megacephala, C. rufifacies* and *L. cuprina* and reported that *C. rufifacies* attain postfeeding stage after 60-70h of hatching.

Kashyap and Pillay (1989a, 1989b) discussed the role of insects in solving crime. They examined and analyzed sixteen insect infested cadavers to evaluate the reliability of entomological method in estimation of time elapsed since death, in relation to other medico legal approaches. Singh and Greenberg (1994) studied survival after submergence in the pupae of five species of blow flies and found that the maximum period of submergence for the pupae after which they could develop into normal adults was four days. These data are potentially useful in estimating duration of submergence of corpse during forensic investigations where the corpse got submerged after pupariation. Nandi (1994) surveyed 19 species of Sarcophagidae under eleven genera and were recorded for the first time from Nagaland, India.

Datta and Parui (1999) studied the Calliphoridae from Meghalaya by reporting 18 species belonging to 3 subfamilies. The Chrysomyinae was represented by 2 species, Calliphorinae by 4 species and Sarcophaginae by 14 species, out of which 3 species were reported only in India. Nandi (2000) reported 19 species of blowflies under 11 genera from Sikkim, India. He also provided distributional records of blowflies from India. Singh and Bharti (2001a) studied the nocturnal oviposition behaviour of three species of blowflies namely: *C. vicina, C. megacephala* and *C. rufifaces.* Singh and Bharti (2001b) also enlisted eight species of ants collected from rabbit carcasses during successional studies in the state of Punjab, India.

Bharti and Singh (2002) also reported the occurrence of larval stages of blow flies during different stages of decay in rabbit carcasses. Nandi (2002) studied biological diversity and distributional records of the species from

West Bengal, India and recorded 41 species of Calliphorid flies. Bharti and Singh (2003) studied the succession of insect communities on rabbit carrion in the state of Punjab, India. They reported 38 species of insects belonging to 13 families from different stages of carrion decay during various seasons of the year. Nandi, (2004) also provided a checklist of 112 species of Calliphoridae of India belonging to 30 genera of 9 subfamilies. Distributional records of the species of all states and union territories were also included in the checklist. Nandi and Sinha (2004) recorded 16 species of muscid flies under 7 genera from Sundarbans Biosphere Reserve and their bionomics and distributional records were also given from India. Singh and Sidhu (2004) studied a checklist of blowflies from North-West India.

Bharti *et al.* (2007) observed the effect of temperature on the development of *C. megacephala* reared in the laboratory at four constant temperatures (22°C, 25°C, 28°C, 30°C). Singh and Bharti (2008) studied nocturnal larviposition by the flesh flies (Diptera: Sarcophagidae). Two species namely: *Sarcophaga albiceps* Meigen and *Sarcophaga hirtipes* Wiedemann were observed to deposit their larvae during night time. Bharti (2009a) listed life tables for two forensically important flies *viz; Ca. vicina* and *Musca domestica nebulo* Fabricius, were generated at varying temperatures. Life history of both *Ca. vicina* and *M. domestica* are temperature dependent. Bharti (2009b) studied medically important flies from India and reported five species of blowflies which are vectors of number of diseases.

Bharti and Kurahash (2010) made a new record of *Lucilia calviceps* Bezzi from India and provided the key to all the Indian species. Bharti (2011) updated checklist of blow flies from India including 120 species from Family Calliphoridae out of which 22 species were endemic.

Rù•ièka *et al.* (2011) recorded eight species of carrion beetles from India. *Nicrophorus melissae* Sikes et Madge, *N. trumboi* Sikes et Madge, and *Thanatophilus porrectus* (Semenov) are reported from India for the first time. *Nicrophorus nepalensis* Hope was reported from Arunachal Pradesh, India for the first time. Distribution of *N. nepalensis* and *Thanatophilus minutus* Kraatz in India is summarized and mapped. Additional recent records of *Nicrophorus encaustus* Fairmaire from Jammu and Kashmir and *Thanatophilus dentiger* (Semenov) from Uttarakhand are provided. A necrophagous association of *N. rufithorax* with carrion of *Semnopithecus entellus* (Dufresne) (Primates: Cercopithecidae) is reported.

Bharti (2012) studied the diversity of blowflies of Himalayan region and correlated the faunal composition with shift in altitude in Himalayan regions. A total of 14 species of which 6 belonging to the genus *Chrysomya*, 2 belonging to the genus *Calliphora* and 6 to the genus *Lucilli* represented the faunal composition on carcass along an elevation gradient in North-West Himalaya.

Sathe and Jadav (2013) studied the diversity of Sarcophagids from Kolhapur District and reported 16 species of Sarcophagids from the region. Sathe *et al.* (2013) recorded diversity of dipterous forensic insects from Kolhapur region, India. They reported 25 species of dipteran flies. Verma and Paul (2013) studied larvae and pupae or empty pupa cases when suitable tissue or other source of information's absent. They studied the effects of commonly abused drugs on growth rates of insects.

Verma (2013) studied the life cycle of *C. rufifacies* under different temperatures *C. rufifacies* showed that its growth cycle was affected by fluctuation in temperatures and these factors can be considered as an estimate of the minimum time of death.

Bharti (2014) first reported *Chrysomya chani* Kurahashi, from India and revised key to the known Indian species of the genus *chrysomya*. Bala and kaur (2014) reported a total of 10 beetle species belonging to 6 families *i.e. Euspilotus assimilis* (Paykull), *Saprinus pensylvanicus* Paykull, *Saprinus sp.* (Histeridae), *Gonocephalum patruele* (Erichson), *Typhaea stercorea* (Linnaeus), *Tenebrio molitor* Linneaus (Tenebrionidae), *D. maculatus* (Dermestidae), *Hybosorus sp.* (Scarabidae), *Pterostichus melanarius* Linneaus (Carabidae) and *Necrobia sp.* (Cleridae). They also observed 2 species from order Hymenoptera *i.e. Camponotus compressus* (Fabricius) and *Pheidole indica* Mayr belonging to family Formicidae during different stages of decomposition. Ramaraj *et al.* (2014) reported the occurrence of dipteran fly, *C. megacephala* for the first time from Royapuram fishing harbour (Chennai), Tamil Nadu, India.

Jadav and Sathe (2015a) recorded a total of 11 species of forensic insects belonging to the orders Diptera (5) and Coleoptera (6). They were associated with carcasses of *Canis domesticus* L. at Kolhapur. Jadav and Sathe (2015b) also reported a total of 22 species of blow flies from Western Ghats of Maharastra, India belonging to nine genera namely: *Silbomya, Calliphora, Phumosia, Melinda, Hemipyrellia, Lucillia, Pollenia, Tainanina* and *Chrysomya*. The dominant genus found in Ghats was *Lucilia* while, *Hemipyrellia* was rarely reported.

Bharti (2015) recorded the new species, *Polleniopsis annamensis* Kurahashi, for the first time in India (Western Ghats). Sharma *et al.* (2015) reviewed the various methods of estimation of post mortem interval using Calliphoridae to make the investigators, law personnel and researchers aware of the importance of entomology in criminal investigations. They also studied the various larval stages of Calliphoridae.

Algalil and Zambare (2015) studied the effect of temperature on the life cycle duration and morphological parameters of different developmental stages of *C. megacephala*.

Review of literature indicates that very little attention is given on forensic insects from Maharashtra except the work of Sathe *et al.* (2013), Sathe and Jadav (2013), Jadav and Sathe (2015a, b), etc.

3 COLLECTION, PRESERVATION AND USE OF FORENSIC INSECTS

Following are the basic essential materials used during the research.

Materials

1. *Sweep net (Fig. 3.1)*: Sweep net was used to collect flying insects. It was made up of a long iron handle of 64cm and steel rim of diameter 30cm. The rim was encircled with net bag with depth of 35cm for collecting insects. Flesh flies, blowflies, hymenopterans, beetles, etc., were collected by this net.
2. *Glass troughs (Fig. 3.2):* Glass troughs measuring 9.5×26cm (height × diameter cm) were used for rearing forensic insects. During the rearing of insects, glass troughs were covered with muslin cloth and secured with rubber bands.
3. *Specimen tube (Fig. 3.3)*: Specimen tubes measuring 9.4 × 3cm (length × diameter cm) were used for temporary storage of adult flies and beetles. The mouth of the tube was covered with muslin cloth/cotton ball for preservation of escape from tubes.
4. *Plastic containers*: Plastic containers of varies size were used for collecting the sample from natural habitat and preparing baits.
5. *Specimen bottles (Fig. 3.4)*: Specimen bottles have a flat bottom and made of strong glass and closed with rubber stopper for prevention of ethanol. Larvae and adults of forensic insects are preserved in it.
6. *Camel hair brushes (Fig. 3.5)*: Camel hair brushes were found to be soft and ideal for handling insects and maggots which were in ethanol and in rearing dishes. Brushes of size no. 1 and no. 5 were used.
7. *Slide boxes (Fig. 3.6)*: Slides boxes measuring 28 mm in length and 22 mm in width were used for keeping microscopic slides of forensic insects.

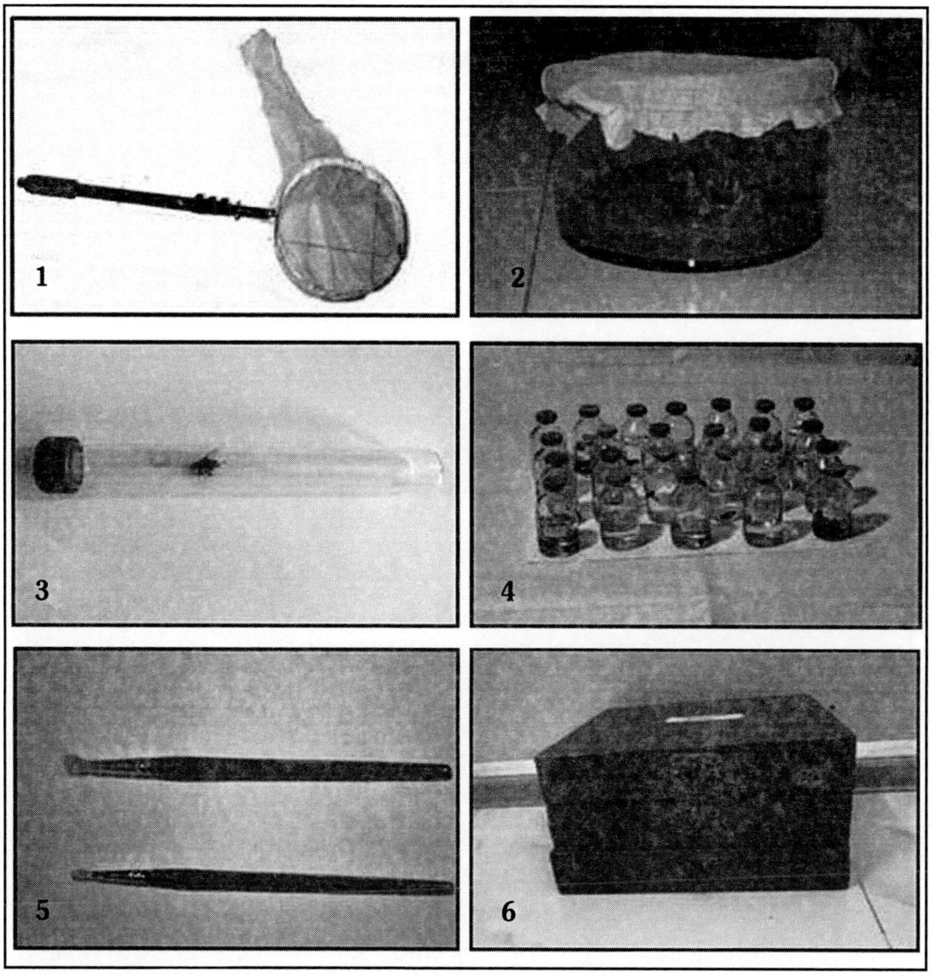

Plate - I: Fig. 3.1: **Sweep net,** Fig. 3.2: **Glass trough,** Fig. 3.3: **Specimen tube,** Fig. 3.4: **Specimen bottles,** Fig. 3.5: **Camel hair brushes,** Fig. 3.6: **Slide boxes.**

8. *Slides and cover slips*: Standard glass slides measuring 7.4 × 2.4 cm and 1mm thick were used. Very small insects and body parts of insects were mounted on slides for close examination under microscope. The specimens were mounted with glass coverslips which were dehydrated first and cleaned in xylene and then mounted in DPX.
9. *Oven (Fig. 3.7):* The oven of size 101 × 70 cm (height x width cm) was used for drying the whole specimens and slides prepared for studies at 60°C for one week.
10. *Store box (Fig. 3.8)*: Store boxes measuring 30.4 × 45.5 × 6.7cm (length × breath × width) were used for storing pinned insects (flies, beetle, etc.).

11. *Compound microscope (Fig. 3.9)*: Compound microscope was used for morphological studies of insects and for measurements of different body parts of the insects.
12. *Light microscope*: Light microscope was used for describing and identifying insect specimens.
13. *Camera (Fig. 3.10):* Nikon D3200 and Sony Coolpix camera was used to take photographs of insects and other materials, whole specimen and microscopic body parts of insects have been photographed.
14. *Entomological pins*: Stainless steel and nickel coated pins of size 00 and 01 were used for pinning specimen. A number 0 size pins were used for pinning flies and number 01 size were used for pinning beetles. A number 0 pin was inserted through the thorax slightly to the right to the middle from ventral side to avoid damaging delicate bristles used for identification for flies. A number 01 size pin was inserted through the right elytron for beetles.
15. *Vernier caliber (Fig. 3.11)*: Vernier caliber was used for measuring insect specimens.
16. *Forceps (Fig. 3.12):* Forceps were used for pinning the insects and handling pinned insects, larvae and pupae during the experiments. Both the blunt and pointed forceps were used.
17. *Rubber gloves (Fig. 3.13):* Rubber gloves were used as precaution while doing collection of insects from the cadavers and in laboratories.
18. *Mask (Fig. 3.14):* It was used for avoiding any type of pathogenic infection from cadaver to scientist/worker.
19. *Knife (Fig. 3.15):* A small knife was used for cutting piece of cadaver along with some stages of forensic insects.
20. *Spoons (Fig. 3.16)*: Steel spoons were used for picking large samples of larvae from the trap and cadaver.
21. *Killing jars (Fig. 3.17):* A heavy, wide mouthed glass jar with a tight fitting stopper was used for temporary keeping of insects and for killing insects.
22. *Rearing cages (Fig. 3.18):* Rearing cages measuring 25 × 25 × 25 cm (height × width × length) were used for rearing forensic insects from egg to larvae and adults.
23. Chemicals used:
    - *(i)* Ethyl acetate;
    - *(ii)* Alcoholic grades (30%,50%, 70%, 90% and Absolute);
    - *(iii)* Xylene and
    - *(iv)* DPX;

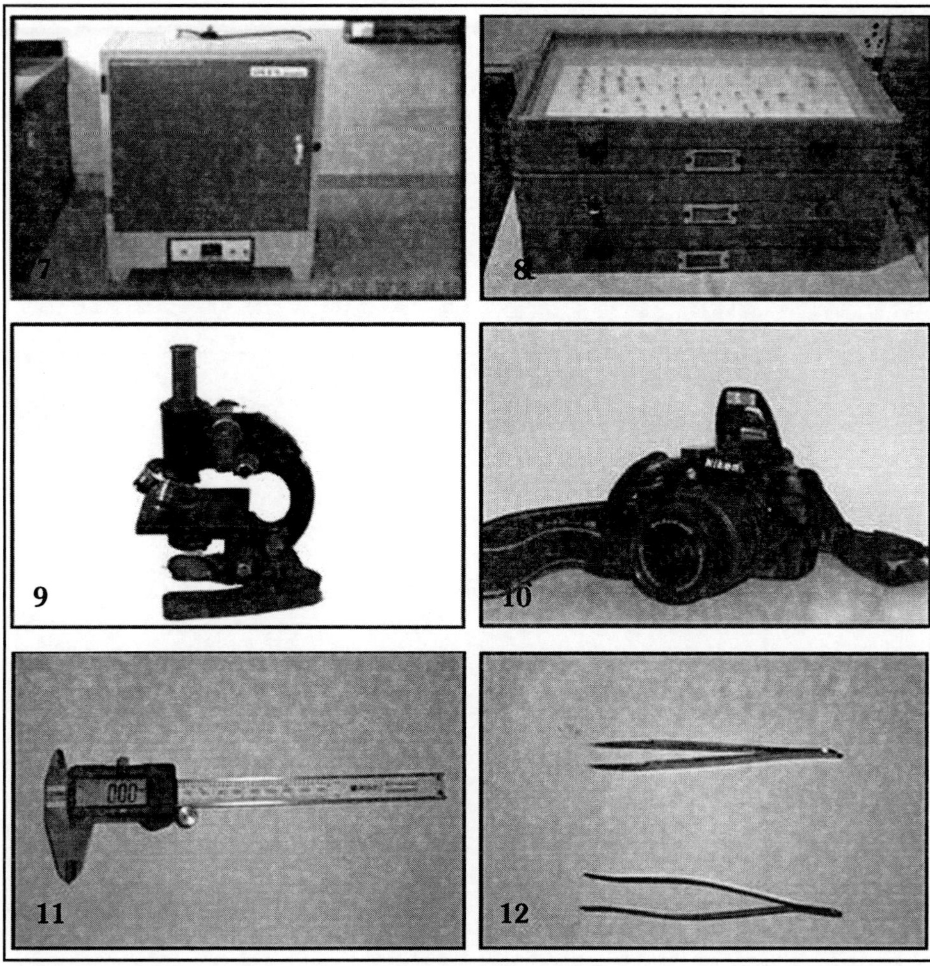

Plate - II: Fig. 3.7: **Oven,** Fig. 3.8: **Store boxes,** Fig. 3.9: **Compound microscope,** Fig. 3.10: **Camera,** Fig. 3.11: **Vernier caliber,** Fig. 3.12: **Foreceps**

Methodology

Study Area

Ten tehsils of Kolhapur district namely: Kagal, Karveer, Panhala, Bhudhargad, Shirol, Hatkanangale, Ajara, Gaganbawada, Radhanagari and Shahuwadi were selected for present study.

Morphological Diversity

Morphological diversity of forensic insects was studied with the help of Light and Compound microscopes. Detailed descriptions of the parts like: head, thorax, abdomen and their appendages have been taken into account for morphological studies. The collected insect specimen has been identified using proper keys and literature cited in bibliography. For preparation of

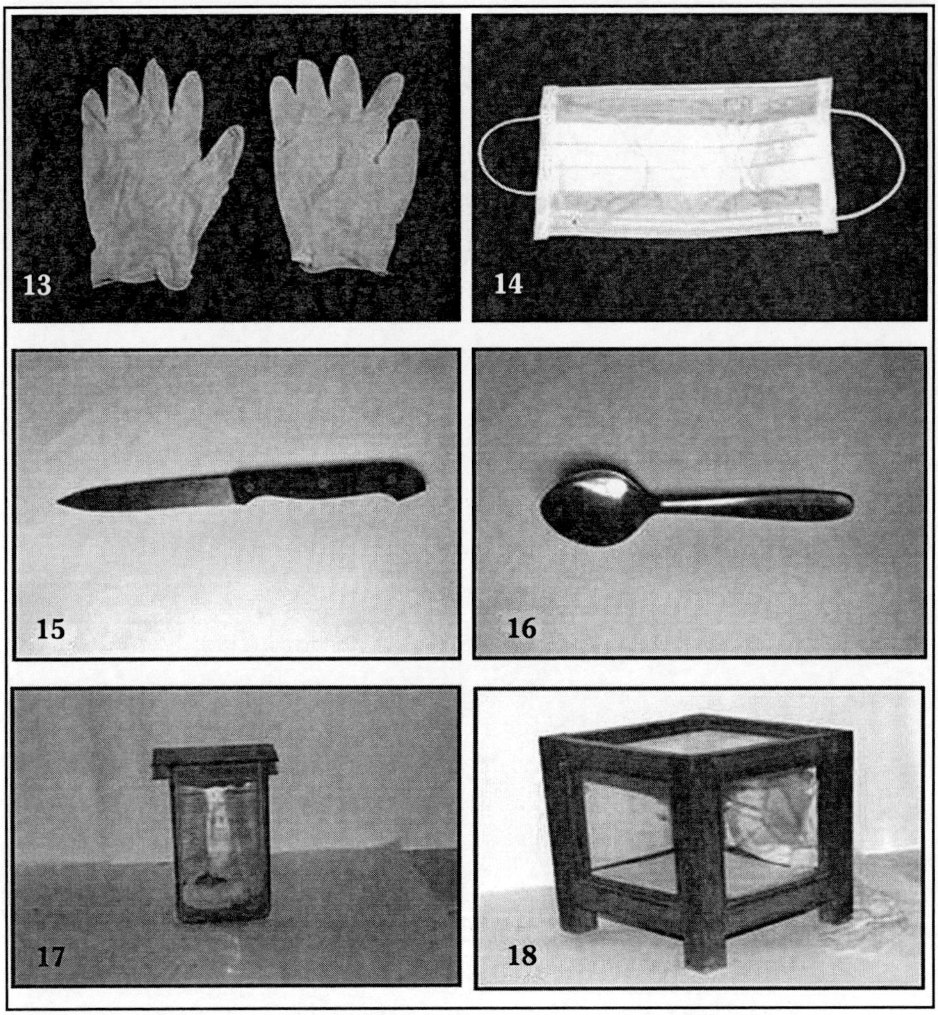

Plate - III: Fig. 3.13:, Fig. 3.14:, Fig. 3.15:, Fig. 3.16:, Fig. 3.17:, Fig. 3.18:.

slides for diversity studies, various body parts and whole insects were taken and dehydrated in alcoholic grades (30%, 50%, 70%, 90% and absolute) and cleared in xylene and mounted in DPX on slide. Measurements of the various body parts were taken in millimeter by using ocular meter. Collection of insects was made by 'One man one hour search method' from the study area at 15 days interval with the help of sweep net (Sathe *et al*. 2014).

Ecological Studies

Seasonal abundance and association of insects with the host/carcasses have been recorded by spot observation/sweep net collection method. The general insect abundance was estimated using two different sampling methods, namely: sweeping net method and bait trap method.

- *Bait traps*: The plastic containers of capacity 500ml and 1000ml with small holes in the lid were baited with meat (purchased from market) of approximately 50gms in random pieces and the container was used as bait. At different spots of collection area, traps were hung on the tree.

Biological Studies

Biology of Forensic insects have been studied under laboratory conditions by providing goat flesh or goat liver for insect in glass rearing cages (25×25×25cm) and glass trough of size 9.5 × 26cm (height × diameter). The glass trough were covered by muslin cloth and secured by rubber band. The development of insects examined from egg laying until pupation and adult formation. The pupae were removed from the carcasses and kept in test tubes for adult emergence. The life cycle of forensic insects was studied by noting the duration of each stage of the insect development *viz*; egg, larva, pupa and adult.

1. *Incubation of egg*: Deposition of egg on carcass to its hatching was the incubation period.
2. *Larval period*: The hatching of egg into larvae and then transformation of them into pupae was the larval period.
3. *Pupal period*: The time from formation of pupae to the formation of adult was counted as pupal period.
4. *Adult longevity*: The time from formation of adult to its death was counted as adult longevity.

- *Rearing on animal tissue*: This method was easiest for laboratory rearing of forensic insects required for research. About 100-200 adults were sufficient to provide a continuous supply of the various life stages for experimental use. Meat/liver was used as food for the forensic insects. The laboratory conditions were 27±1° C, 75-80 per cent RH and 12hr photoperiod for development and quick turnover of the life cycle.
- *Rearing of flies*: The rearing was done in a well-ventilated room maintained at above said conditions.
- *Maintenance of adults*: Adults were hold in glass cages (25 × 25 × 25cm) with a nylon netting sleeve secured with a rubber band at one end. Adults were fed with dry sugar crystals *ad libitum* in a Petri dish, and water with a cotton wick. Bovine liver was provided for about 12 hours during the dark period for oviposition. Some 50-60 flies were kept in each cage, and 2 or 3 cages were maintained so as to provide for a continuous supply of eggs. The oviposited eggs in batches were collected and transferred to larval rearing cages.

- *Rearing of larvae*: The larvae were reared on beef liver replenished as needed in ventilated clear glass troughs 9.5 × 26cm (height × diameter). Vermiculite or untreated sawdust 1-2cm deep was provided for pupation of mature larvae at the base of the glass troughs. The rearing glass troughs were kept covered by muslin cloth so that mature larvae do not escape. Pupae were collected and transferred to plastic containers perforated with small holes for aeration to insect. The adults were emerged in plastic containers. Thus, sufficient number of adults were collected and recycled for developmental studies from egg to adult.

How Insects are used in Forensic Science?

1. *Oviposition pattern:* Egg laying or oviposition pattern of forensic insects helps in detecting the exact time of death. The incubation period is taken into account for counting the exact time of death of a person.
2. *Larval forms and their association:* The insects have egg, larval, pupal and adult stage in their life cycle. The larvae develop on specific host and with specific time duration. Within the larvae there are different instars as 2,3 and 5 in different species. Therefore, the larval association and the period in total and larval period of specific instars help counting the exact time of death.
3. *Pupal forms and their association:* Many forensic insects pupate outside the dead body or some pupate beneath or under the dead body. The behaviours of pupation in insects are helpful for detecting the exact time of death. Pupae also help in detecting probable place of the dead body. Therefore type of pupa and its staying duration is used in counting the time of death.
4. *Adult forms and their association*: A very large number of insects are visualized as forensic insects. The dead bodies have 8 stages of decomposition. Every stage has its own insect diversity. Thus, noting the association of insects on specific stage of decomposition, the time of death of a person can be easily detectable. The sequence of occurrence of insects on dead body also places important role in time detection. Fleshflies and blowflies come very first on carcasses or cadaver, the beetle comes second, later, the lepidopterans and parasitic insects join the carcass environment for their association for development on carcass or parasitizition on forensic insects feeding on carcass. Therefore, the correct identification of forensic insects, their collection, preservation and obtaining clues have tremendous importance in forensic science.
5. *Environmental conditions in which the death occurred*: Certain insects have their own and specific environment to survive, grow and to reproduce. Thus the insects help us in explaining the type of environment where the death was occurred. Since many insects have their specific zones of temperature and humidity for survival, development, longevity and

reproduction activities. Their development and survival is restricted in certain specific environment or specific ecosystems. Thus their association with dead body and existing environment help in obtaining appropriate clues in forensic science.

6. *The route followed by the culprit during crime*: The insects have specific association with flora planted at road side. During the transportation, if the vehicle is used, it can bleated by the flying insects associated with such flora. The residual body part of the insects attached to the vehicle will help in identification of insects, their association with flora and the characteristic of road flora. This will help in identified the route used by the culprit during the crime.
7. *Whether the death occurred was due to poison of insect origin*: There are several poisonous insects (Sathe *et al.* 2011) which causes fatal effects on human being. The insects help in avoiding the confusion with poisoning caused by either insects or other poisons. Blister beetle, Natada and some other caterpillars, ants, wasps, honey bees, etc., have their own poison. They have their own characteristic features. Thus, they will help in avoiding confusion in different poisons and insect poisons. The induced poisons are saturated in various organs of insects including tissues if they develop on poisoned cadaver. Such poisons are posed to detect and quantify experimental in the laboratory with the help of insects.
8. *Insects help at disfiguring stage*: The insects feed on dead body and they disfigure the cadaver many times in a characteristic of month but, disfiguring of the dead body is also possible with other reasons and becomes difficult to identify the dead body. In such cases, their characteristic distinction of carcass or cadaver helps in avoiding confusion and obtaining appropriate clues.

4 DIVERSITY OF FORENSIC INSECTS

INTRODUCTION

Insects are richest group of animal kingdom and plays very important role in ecology, ethology, embryology, genetics and many applied sciences including: forensic science. Forensic science is involved in identification of various types of forensic insects and their developmental and ethological studies related to carcasses and cadavers. They have association with humans, cattle's and several domesticated animals and have host specificity in several cases. Their association and the development helps in forensic science for detecting exact time of death of a person. The insects also help to detect the road used by the culprit in murder case. The dead body has 8 stages of decomposition and every stage has its peculiarity with respect to diversity of insects. Therefore, in the present study diversity of forensic insect have been studied.

Review of literature indicates that White as Senior White (1940), James (1947), Putman (1977), Smith (1986), Greenberg (1991), Cross key and Lane (1993), Kurahashi and Thapa (1994), Stevens and Wall (1997), Smith and Wall (1997), Anderson (2001), Byrd and Castner (2001), Dadour *et al.* (2001), Kurahashi (2001), Kurahashi and Chowanadisai (2001), Tachibana and Numata (2001), Nandi (2004), Bharti and Singh (2003), Grassberger *et al.* (2003), Pitts and Wall (2004), Singh and Sidhu (2004, 2007), Kimberly (2005), Ronges (2005, 2009), Clark *et al.* (2006), Bharti (2009, 2012), Bharti and Kurahashi (2010), Higley and Haskel (2010), Shiravi *et al.* (2011), Vasconcelos *et al.* (2012), Sathe *et al.* (2013), Sathe and Jadav (2013, 2014), Vasconcelos *et al.* (2013), Ghodake *et al.* (2014), Jadav and Sathe (2014,2015), etc.,) worked on diversity of forensic insects.

Materials and Methods

Diversity of forensic insects have been studied by collecting the insects found on carcasses of various types of animals found in Kolhapur district both in forest and plain regions. The insects have been collected with the help of insect net and sometimes with the help of plastic containers. Many times pieces of carcass have been collected from the natural habitat and reared in the laboratory at a 27± 1°C, 75 to 80 per cent RH and 12 hour photoperiod. Collected insects have been pinned and dried at 60° C in drying chamber. For details of morphological feature slides of wings and legs have also been prepared. The insects have been described morphological by taking into account of body parts like: head, thorax, abdomen and their appendages. The insects have been identifying by consulting appropriate literature cited in bibliography.

Morphological Considerations

Morphological considerations and terminology adopted in describing dipterous flies and beetles are represented in Figs. 4.1 to 4.9.

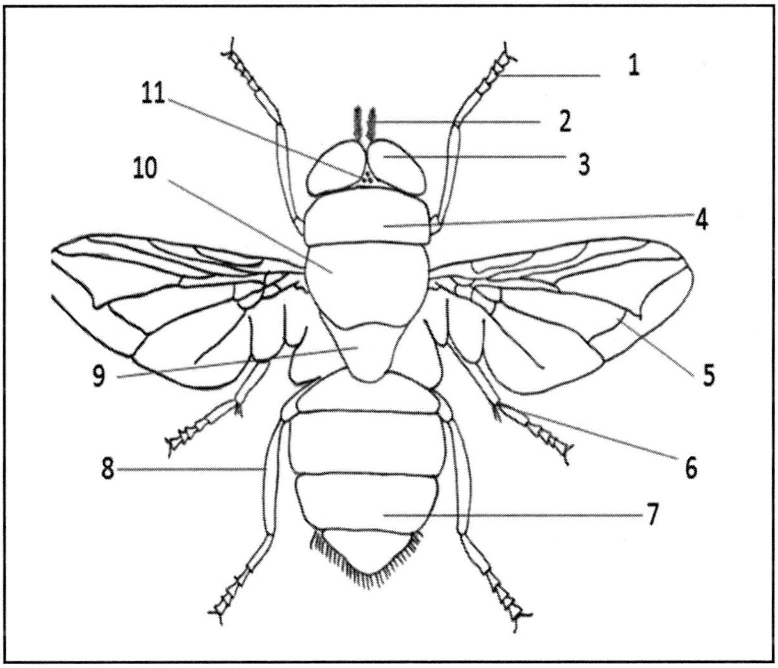

Fig. 4.1: **Blow fly-dorsal view:** 1 - **Foreleg,** 2 - **Antenna,** 3 - **Compound eyes,** 4 - **Occellar triangle, 5** - **Wing,** 6 - **Mid leg,** 7 - **Abdomen,** 8 - **Hind leg,** 9 - **Scutellum,** 10 - **Scutum,** 11 - **prescutem**

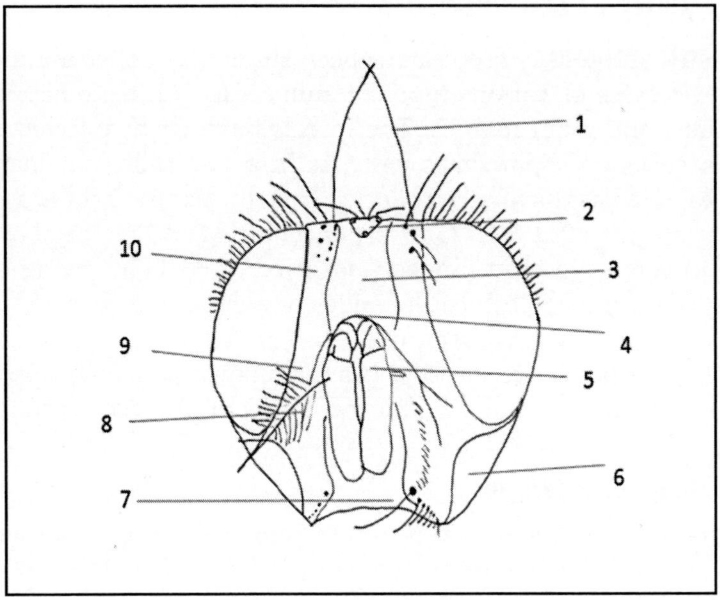

Fig. 4.2: **Blow fly-head:** 1 - **Post verticles,** 2 - **Ocellar triangle,** 3 - **Frontal vittae,** 4 - **Lunule,** 5 - **Antenna,** 6 - **Genaldialation,** 7 - **vibrissa,** 8 - **Arista,** 9 - **Parafacial,** 10 - **Para frontalia**

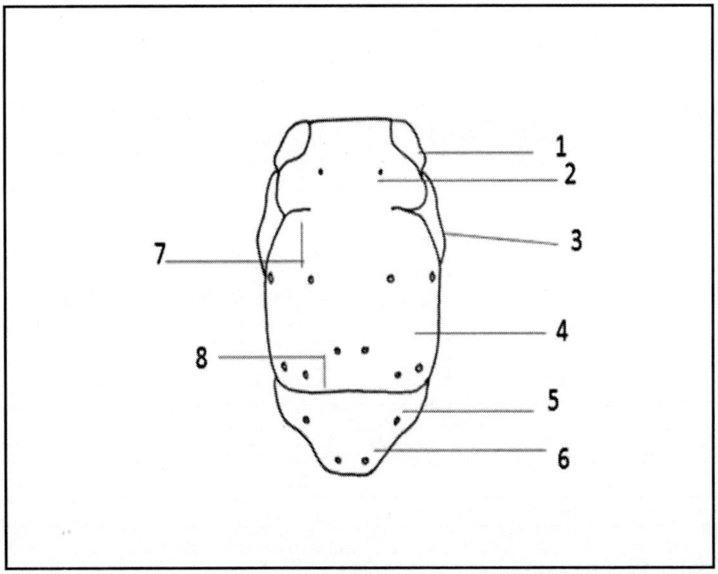

Fig. 4.3: **Blow fly-dorsal view of thorax:** 1 - **Post - pronotum,** 2 - **Prescu tum,** 3 - **Presutaral supra-alar,** 4 - **Scutellum,** 5 - **Scutum,** 6 - **Apical setae,** 7 - **Transverrsatwru,** 8 - **Intal alar**

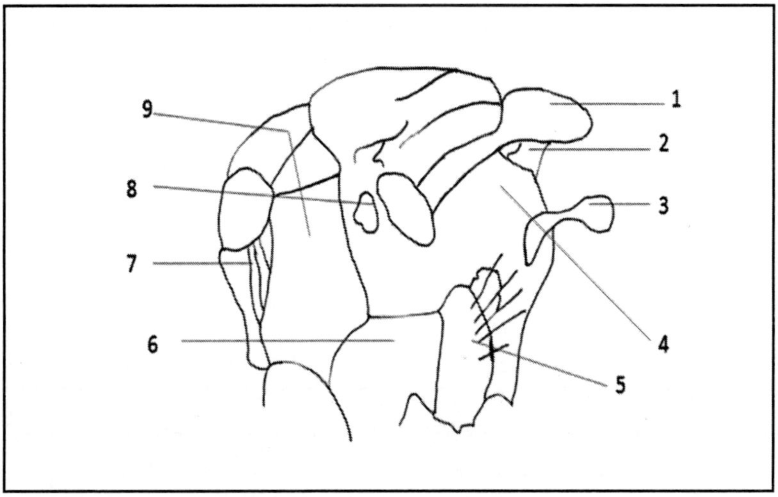

Fig. 4.4: **Blow fly-lateral view thorax:** 1 - **Scutellum,** 2 - **Post scutellum,** 3 - **Haltar,** 4 - **Supra squamal ridge,** 5 - **Hypopleron,** 6 - **Sternopleuron,** 7 - **Antherior thoracic spiracle,** 8 - **Greater ampulla,** 9 - **Mesopleuron**

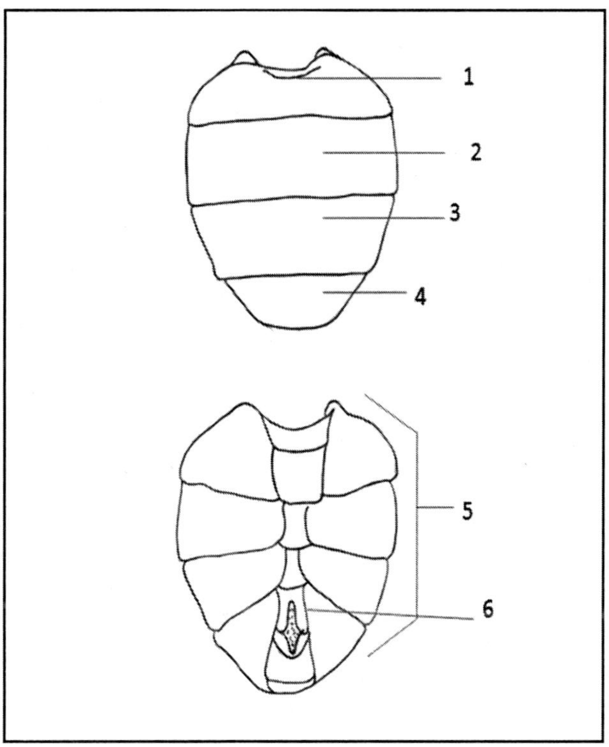

Fig. 4.5: **Blow fly-abdomen:** A - **Dorsal view:** 1-1+2 **tergite,** 2-3rd **tergite,** 4-4th **tergite.** B - **ventral view:** 5 - **strenites,** 6 - **Male genitalia**

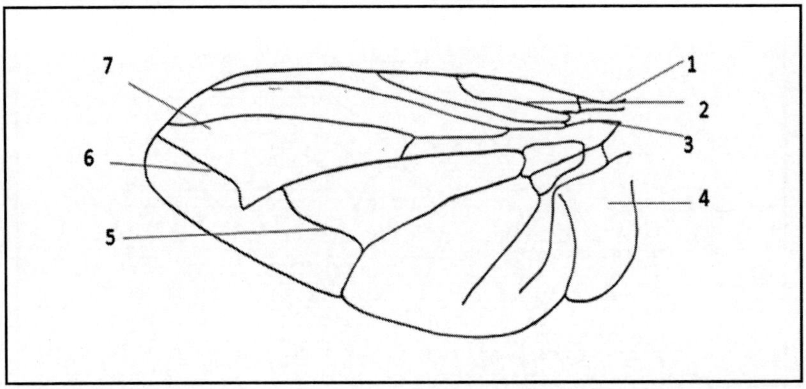

Fig. 4.6: **Blow fly-wing:** 1 - **Tegula,** 2 - **Coastal cell,** 3 - **Stem vein,** 4 - **Alula,** 5 - **Lower marginal cross vein,** 6 - **Upper marginal cross vein,** 7 - **Third longitudinal vein**

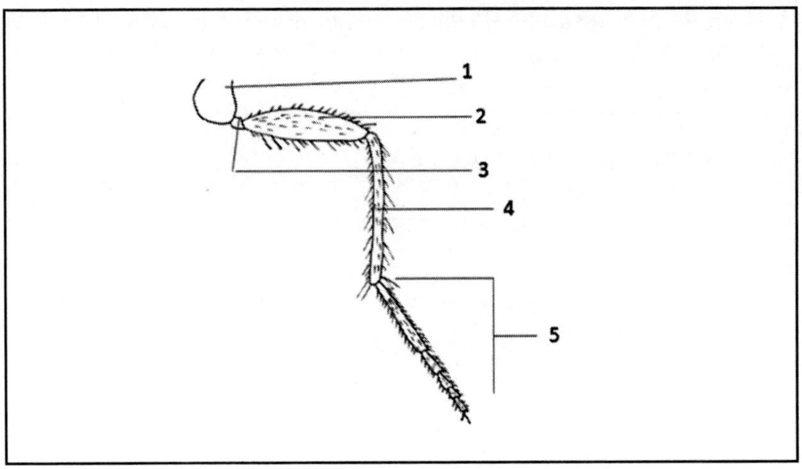

Fig. 4.7: **blow fly-fore leg:** 1 - **coxa,** 2 - **Femur,** 3 - **Trochanter,** 4 - **Tibia,** 5 - **Tarsus**

RESULTS

Family Calliphoridae

This Family is Characterised by:

1. Mostly robust medium to large sized flies, partly or wholly metallic blue or green, sometimes polished black or dull brassy, occasionally small, slender, and without metallic sheen.
2. Male holoptic with upper eye facets not much enlarged.
3. Frons always narrower than in female.
4. Sexes differ with leg chaetotaxy and body color.

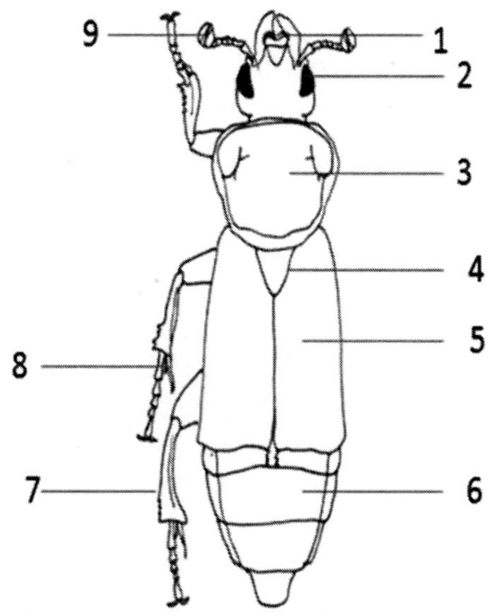

Fig. 4.8: **Beetle-dorsal view:** 1 - **Mandible,** 2 - **Eye,** 3 - **Pronotum,** 4 - **Scutellum,** 5 - **Elytra,** 6 - **Abdominal tergite,** 7 - **Tibia,** 8 - **Spurs,** 9 - **Antenna**

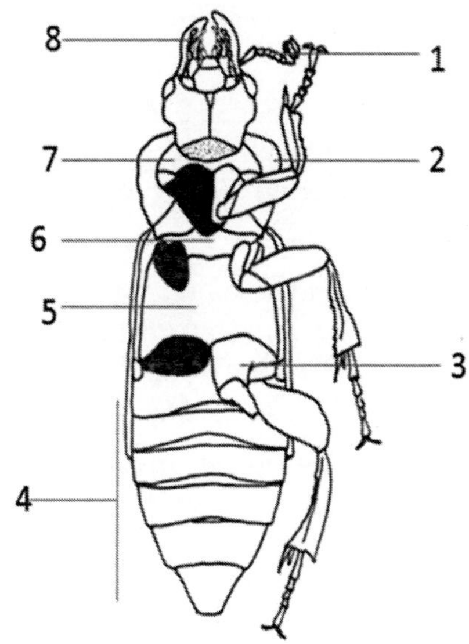

Fig. 4.9: **Beetle-ventral view:** 1 - **Antenna,** 2 - **Epipleuron,** 3 - **Coxa,** 4 - **Abdominal sternites,** 5 - **Metasternum,** 6 - **Mesosternum,** 7 - **Prosternum,** 8 - **Maxillary palp**

Subfamily Chrysomyiinae

Characters

1. The flies are all metallic in coloration.
2. Presence of hairs on the stem vein of the wing and the presence of fine hairs on some portion of the upper surface of the lower calypter.
3. Individual found only in tropical and subtropical climates and more or less replace, ecologically, the common blow-flies, calliphora, of more temperate regions. The subfamily is represented by only one genus *Chrysomya* from the Oriental region.

Genus Chrysomya *Robineau-desvoidy*, 1830

This genus is characterised by stiff erect setae on greater ampulla and dorsum of first and second abdominal tergite black, posterior margins of abdominal tergite 3 and 4 black. Twelve species from this genus have been reported.

Key to the Indian species of the genus *Chrysomya* (Bharti, 2014)

1. Prothoracic spiracle white/yellow 2

   – Prothoracic spiracle black to dark brown 5
2. Only one sternopleural bristle developed, 0+1 ...... *C. nigripes* Aubertin, 1932

   – Two sternopleural bristles developed, 1+1 3
3. Prostigmatic bristle present 4

   – Prostigmatic bristle absent........................ *C. albiceps* (Wiedmann, 1819)
4. Mesopleural bristles 5, acrostichal 0+1, dorsocentral 2+2, acrophallu sunstalked projecting anteriorly .... *C. rufifacies* (Macquart, 1843)

   – Mesopleural bristles 6, acrostichal 0+2, dorsocentral 3+3, acrophallus wide stalked projecting posteriorly .... *C. indica* Nandi, 2004
5. Femora swollen in male and female, but more noticeably so in male, eyes dichoptic in both sexes; outer-vertical well developed in male, female tergite 5 with medial cleft posteriorly, facial ridge developed .... *C. villeneuvi* Patton, 1922

   – Femora normal, eyes holoptic in male or dichoptic in both sexes; female tergite 5 with or without median cleft posteriorly, facial ridge normal 6
6. Alar and thorasicsquamae both entirely fuscous black, parafacialia and genae fuscous 7

   – At least base of alar squamae white 8

7. Body blue to purple, post gena usually covered with yellowish hairs; length of genae in profile more than that of eye height, height of gena compared to total head about 3/10 in male and about 4/10 in female; male cerci elongate, approximately 3×length of surstylli .... *C. pinguis* (Walker, 1856)

   – Body dark green; post gena usually covered with black and brown hairs; gena in profile same length as eye; height of gena compare to total head about 2/10 in male, about 3/10 in female; male cerci stout, not more than 2×length of surstylli .... *C. defixa* (Walker, 1856)

8. Parafacialia and genae fuscous to black; setulae and hairs on parafacialia and facialia blackish; venter of tergite 5 with black hairs only; basal part of alar squama opaque white, bare ventrally except for fringe .... *C. chani* Kurahashi, 1979

   – Parafacialia and genae entirely orange; setulae and hairs on the parafacialia and facialia yellowish; venter of tergite 5 intermixed with yellow hairs; opaque white basal part of alar squama haired ventrally 9

9. Squamae white; facets of male eye somewhat enlarged above, but not sharply demarcated from area of smaller facets below; frontal side of female parallel-sided .... *C. bezziana* Villeneuve, 1914

   – Squamae largely brown except for the pale base; facets of male eye much enlarged above, sharply demarcated from area of the smaller facets below; frontal stripe of female broader at middle of frons, not parallel-sided ....*C. megacephala* (Fabricius, 1794)

Chrysomya nigripes Aubertin, 1932

(Plate - I: Figs. 4.10-4.14) (See Page no. 35)

- *Male* (Fig. 4.10-4.11): Body long 5.34mm, wide 2.75mm; wing 5.31mm long and 2.19mm wide; antenna 0.59mm long, 0.24mm broad; thorax 2.94mm long, 1.74mm broad; abdomen 1.17mm long, 2.75mm broad; foreleg 4.46mm long, black.
- *Head* (Fig. 4.12): 1.55mm long and 2.44mm broad, black; compound eyes reddish in colour with 0.35mm long and 1.35mm wide; frontal wide 0.52mm; parafrontalia grayish to blackish towards the vertex with black setae; frontal vittae brown; parafacialia and gena grey with pale hairs; a pair of fronto orbitals; vibrissa and subvibrissalsetule black; palpi black with black setae.
- *Antenna*: 0.59mm long, 0.24mm wide; brownish; scape black 0.02mm long, 0.04mm wide; pedicel dark brown 0.16mm long, 0.20mm wide, first flagellomere dark brown 0.41mm long, 0.24mm wide; Arista plumose.

- *Flagellar Formula:* S L/W: 0.5 , P L/W: 0.8 , F L/W: 1.7 , A: 1.
- *Thorax*: Metallic shining bluish purple; 2.94mm long, 1.74mm broad; prescutum- 0.88mm long, 1.74mm wide; scutum- 1.23mm long, 1.74mm wide, scutellum- 0.83mm long, 1.21mm in wide; greater ampulla with short black; anterior thoracic spiracle dark brown; proepimeral setae present; acrostical setae 0+1; dorsocentral setae 2+2 ; intra-alar setae 1; postalar setae 2; supra-alar setae 2; presutural intra alar absent; humeral setae 2; anepisternal setae; apical setae 2; subapical setae 2; distal scutellar setae 2.
- *Wing* (Fig. 4.13): 5.31mm long and 2.19mm wide; stem vein setose; basicosta dark brown with short hairs and 2 long setae; upper calypter white transparent; lower calypter smoky brown with long black setae, margin dark.
- *Halter:* Light brown with brown knob.
- *Fore leg* (Fig. 1.14): Black to brownish; 4.46mm long, coxa 0.69 mm long, trochanter 0.27 mm long, femur 1.56 mm long, tibia 1.28 mm long, tarsus 0.66 mm long.
- *Abdomen*: 1.17mm long and 2.75mm wide; metallic blue shining with 1st and 2nd tergites black; posterior margins of the 3rd and 4th tergites black banded; presence of setae.
- *Genitalia:* Terminalia round, orange, densely covered with short setae at the end. 1-3 sternites are quadrangular.
- *Host plant:* unknown.
- *Paratype:* 7 male, 9 female, coll. Divya Jadav. Feb.-May, wing and legs on slide, Pinned insects, labeled as above.
- *Distribution:* 1 male, Gaganbawda, 26-II-2014; 2 male, Shirol, 04-II-2014; 4 male Radhanagari, 25-IX-2014; 3 female, Gaganbawda, 26-II-2014; 6 female, Shirol, 04-II-2014.

Chrysomya rufifacies **(Macquart, 1843)**
(Plate - II: Figs. 4.15-4.21)

- *Male* (Fig. 4.15-4.16): Body long 9.36mm, wide 3.67mm; wing 7.41mm long and 2.40mm wide; antenna 1.37mm long, 0.30mm broad; thorax 4.21mm long, 3.35mm broad; foreleg 7.06 mm long, black; abdomen 3.00mm long, 3.67mm broad; hind leg mm long.
- *Head* (Fig. 4.17): 3.25mm long and 3.44mm broad, orange; compound eyes reddish in colour with 2.37mm long and 1.21mm wide, separated, facets are small and uniform; frontal wide 1.20 mm; parafrontalia blackish towards the vertex and silvery towards parafacial with black setae; frontal

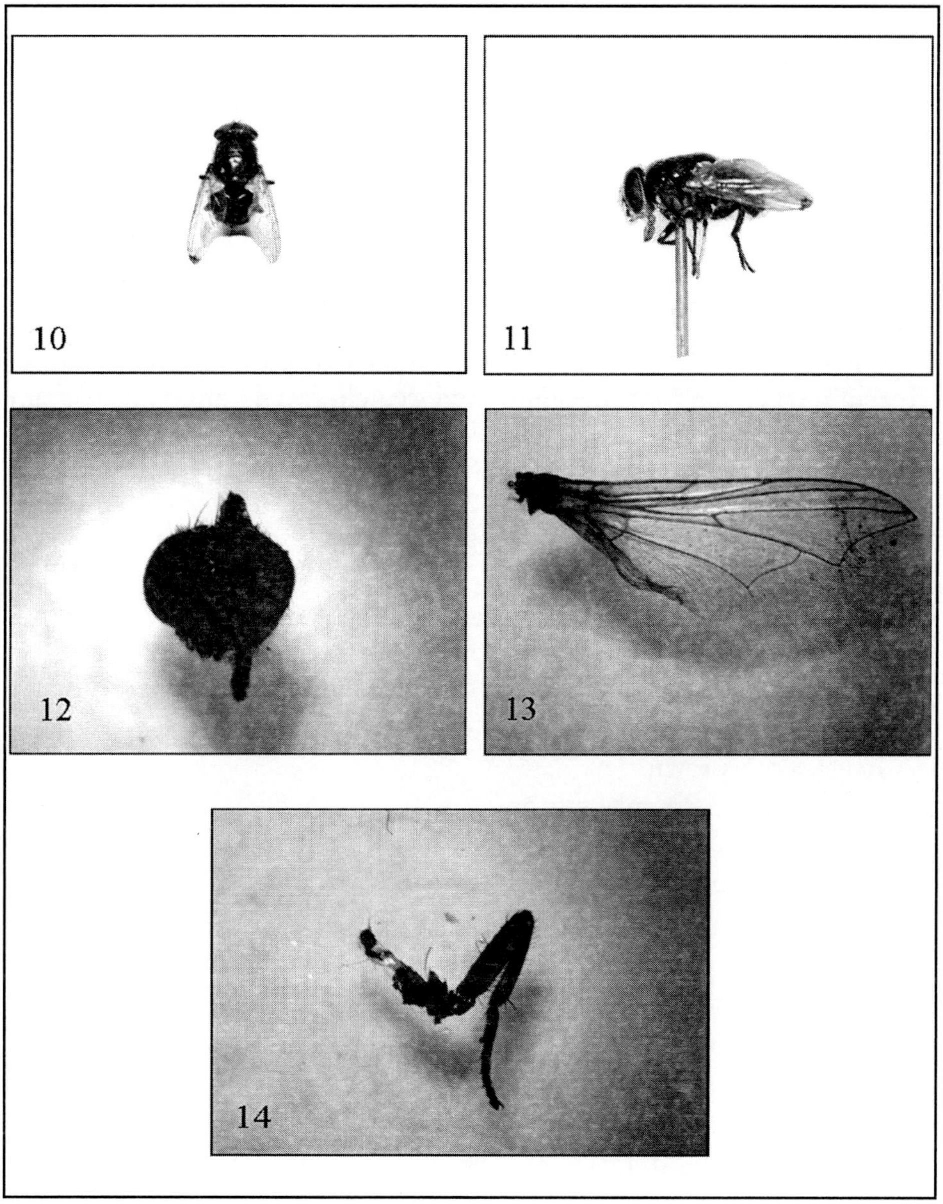

Plate - I: *C. nigripes* (10-14): Fig. 4.10: **Adult-dorsal view,** Fig. 4.11: **Adult-lateral view,** Fig. 4.12: **Head,** Fig. 4.13: **Wing,** Fig. 4.14: **Fore leg**

vittae more brownish towards lunule and blackish towards vertex; parafacialia and gena yellowish with golden hairs; a pair of fronto orbitals; vibrissa and subvibrissal setule black; palpi yellow with black setae.

- *Antenna*: 1.37mm long, 0.30mm wide; dark brown; scape black 0.04mm long, 0.07mm wide; pedicle dark brown 0.44mm long, 0.25mm wide, first flagellomere dark brown 0.89mm long, 0.30mm wide; arista plumose.
- *Flagellar Formula*: S L/W: 0.57, P L/W: 1.76, F L/W: 2.97, A: 1.77.
- *Thorax*: Metallic green shining with purple reflections; 4.21mm long, 3.35mm broad; prescutum 1.21mm long, 3.35mm wide, more silvery dusting towards the head than towards scutum with 2 grey stripe; scutum 1.83mm long, 3.35mm wide, scutellum 1.17mm long, 1.44mm wide; greater ampulla with short black; anterior thoracic spiracle white; proepimeral setae present; acrostical setae 0+1; dorsocentral setae 2+; intra-alar setae 1; postalar setae 2; supra-alar setae 2; presutural intra alar absent; humeral setae 2; anepisternal setae 3; apical setae 2; subapical setae 2; distal scutellar setae 2.
- *Wing* (Fig. 4.18): 7.41mm long and 2.40mm wide; stem vein setose; basicosta dark brown with short hairs and 2 long setae; upper calypter white transparent with pale hairs and creamy margin; lower calypter white with golden hairs, margin dark.
- *Halter*: Dark brown.
- *Fore leg* (Fig. 4.19): Black; 7.06mm long; coxa 0.99 mm long brownish with golden setae; trochanter 0.39 mm long dark brown; femur 1.67mm long black; tibia 2.49 mm long; tarsus 1.52mm long.
- *Abdomen* (Fig. 4.20-4.21): 3.00mm long and 3.67mm wide; metallic blue shining with 1st and 2nd tergites black with green reflections; posterior margins of the 3rd and 4th tergites black banded; presence of setae.
- *Genitalia:* Terminalia round, orange, densely covered with short setae at the end; 1-3 sternites are quadrangular.
- *Host plant:* unknown.
- *Paratype:* 7 male, 10 female, coll. Divya Jadav. Jan.-Dec., wing and legs on slide, pinned insects, labelled as above.
- *Distribution:* 1 male, Kolhapur, 10-III-2014; 1 male, Shirol, 04-II-2014; 4 male, Ajara, 21-V-2014; 1 male, Radhanagari, 19-XII-2014; 3 female, Kolhapur, 10-III-2014; 3 female, Shirol, 04-II-2014; 4 female, Ajara, 21-V-2014.

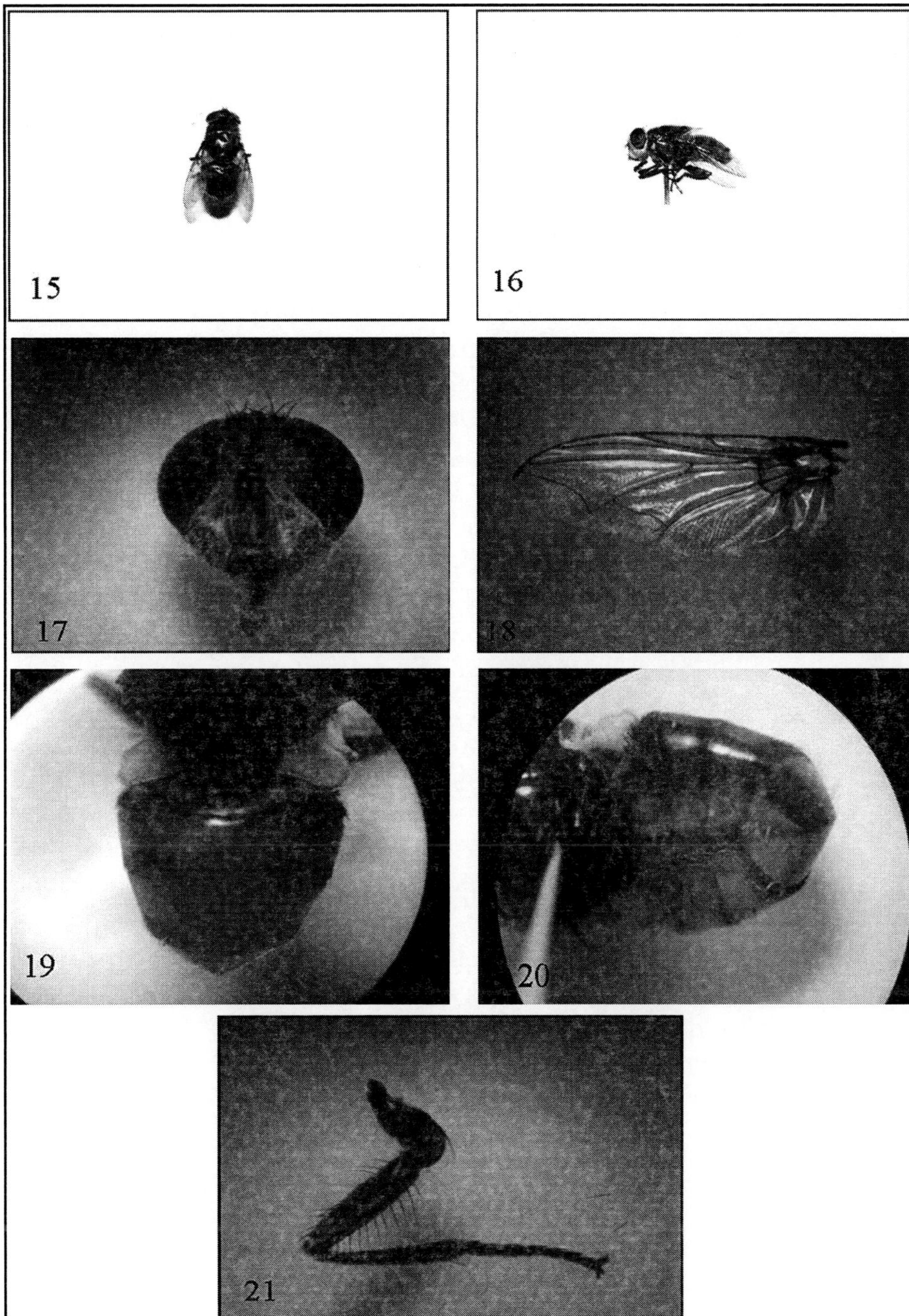

Plate – II: ***C.rufifacies*** (15-21): Fig. 4.15: **Adult-dorsal view,** Fig. 4.16: **Adult-lateral view,** Fig. 4.17: **Head,** Fig. 4.18: **Wing,** Fig. 4.19: **Abdomen dorsal view,** Fig. 4.20: **Abdomen ventral view,** Fig. 4.21: **Fore leg**

Chrysomya villeneuvi Patton
(Plate - III: Figs. 4.22-4.26)

- *Male* (Fig. 4.22-4.23): Body long 9.67mm, wide 3.50mm; wing 8.22mm long and 3.19mm wide; antenna 1.64mm long, 0.46mm broad; thorax 4.72mm long, 3.50mm broad; abdomen 4.70mm long, 3.88mm broad; foreleg 8.60mm long, black.
- *Head* (Fig.4.24): 3.45mm long and 3.24mm broad, orange; compound eyes reddish in colour with 2.56mm long and 1.55mm wide, eye facets small and uniform; frontal wide 1.05mm; parafrontalia black towards the vertex and silvery towards parafacial; frontal vittae black; parafacialia black covered with silvery to mentem; gena grey with golden hairs; a pair of fronto orbitals; vibrissa and subvibrissal setule black; palpi orange.
- *Antenna*: 1.64mm long, 0.46mm wide; yellow to orange with brownish ends at the tips of first flagellomere; scape 0.04mm long orange, 0.06mm wide; pedicel orange tips 0.59mm long, 0.18mm wide, first flagellomere dark brown 1.01mm long, 0.46mm wide; arista plumose.
- *Flagellar Formula*: S L/W: 0.67, P L/W: 3.27, F L/W: 2.19, A: 2.04.
- *Thorax*: Metallic shining green to purple; 4.72mm long, 3.50mm broad; prescutum- 1.46mm long, 3.50mm wide, more silvery dusting towards the head than towards scutum with 2 grey stripe; scutum- 1.91mm long, 3.50mm wide, scutellum- 1.35mm long, 2.37mm wide; greater ampulla with short black; anterior thoracic spiraclepale brown; proepimeral setae present; acrosticalsetae 0+1; dorsocentral setae 2+2 ; intra-alar setae 1; postalar setae 2; supra-alar setae 2; presutural intra alar absent; humeral setae 3; anepisternal setae 3; apical setae 2; subapical setae 2; distal scutellar setae 2.
- *Wing* (Fig. 4.25): 8.22mm long and 3.19mm wide; entirely transparent; stem vein setose; basicosta dark brown with short hairs and 2 long setae; upper part of upper calypter transparent, light brown margin while lower part non transparent with white margin; lower calypter creamy with black setae, margin dark.
- *Halter*: Light brown to yellow with brown knob.
- *Fore leg* (Fig. 4.26): Dark brown; 8.60mm long; coxa 1.30mm long brownish with golden setae; trochanter 0.44 mm long shinny black; femur 2.22 mm long metallic blue reflections; tibia 2.52 mm long; tarsus 2.12 mm long; femora and tibia swollen.
- *Abdomen*: 4.70mm long and 3.88mm wide; oval; metallic blue shining with 1st and 2nd tergites black; posterior margins of the 3rd and 4th tergites black banded; presence of setae.

- *Genitalia:* Terminalia round, metallic green covered with short setae at the end. 1-3 sternite are quadrangular.
- *Host plant:* unknown.
- *Paratype:* 7 male, 11 female, coll. Divya Jadav. Mar.-Dec., wing and legs on slide, Pinned insects, labeled as above.
- *Distribution:* 1 male, Gaganbawda, 08-III-2014; 3 male, Ajara, 17-VI-2014; 2 male, Kolhapur, 24-XII-2014; 1 male, Radhanagari, 11-XII-2014;3 female, Gaganbawda, 08-III-2014; 2 female, Ajara, 17-VI-2014; 1 female, Kolhapur, 24-XII-2014; 5 female, Radhanagari, 11-XII-2014.

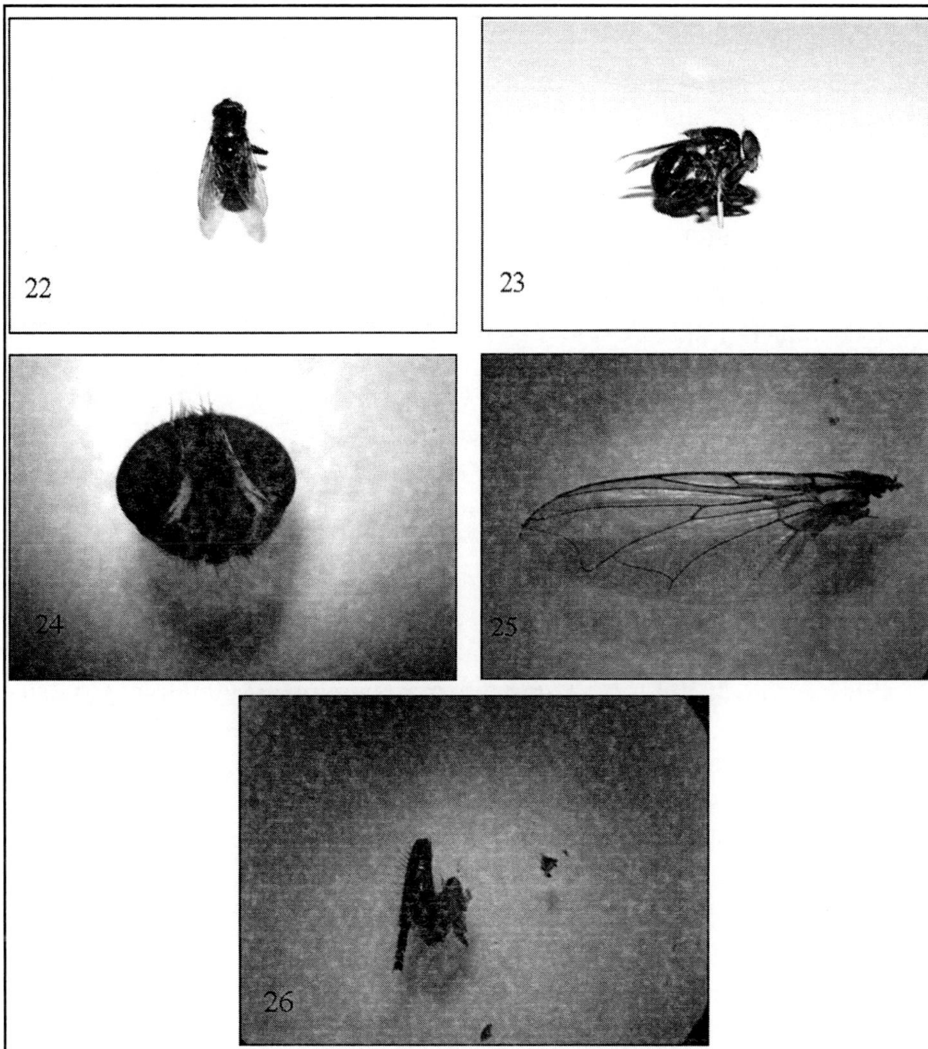

Plate – III *C. villeneuvi* (22-26): Fig. 4.22: **Adult-dorsal view,** Fig. 4.23: **Adult-lateral view,** Fig. 4.24: **Head,** Fig. 4.25: **Wing,** Fig. 4.26: **Fore leg**

Chrysomya indica Nandi, 2004 (Plate - IV: Figs. 4.27-4.31)

- *Male* (Fig. 4.27-4.28): Body long 4.44 mm, wide 2.72mm; wing 6.04 mm long and 2.15mm wide; antenna 0.89mm long, 0.21mm broad; thorax 4.09mm long, 2.72mm broad; abdomen 2.23mm long, 3.10mm broad; foreleg 6.56mm long, black.
- *Head* (Fig. 4.29): 2.22mm long and 2.56mm broad, creamy; compound eyes reddish in colour with 2.01mm long and 1.40mm wide; frontal wide 0.10mm; parafrontalia reduced to a line; frontal vittae absent; parafacialia and gena creamy yellow with golden hairs; vibrissa black; subvibrissal setule pale yellow; palpi orange with black setae.
- *Antenna*: 0.89mm long, 0.21mm wide; scape black 0.03mm long, 0.04mm wide; pedicel dark brown 0.39mm long, 0.19mm wide, first flagellomere dark brown 0.47mm long, 0.21mm wide; arista plumose.
- *Flagellar Formula*: S L/W: 0.75, P L/W: 2.05, F L/W: 2.23, A: 1.67.
- *Thorax:* Metallic shining bluish purple; 4.09mm long, 2.72mm broad; prescutum 1.16mm long, 2.72mm in wide; scutum- 1.38mm long, 2.72mm wide, scutellum- 1.15mm long, 1.88mm wide; greater ampulla with short black; anterior thoracic spiracle white; proepimeral setae present; acrostical setae 0+1; dorsocentral setae 2+1; intra-alar setae 1; postalar setae 2; supra-alar setae 2; presutural intra alar absent; humeral setae 3; anepisternal setae 3; apical setae 2; subapical setae 2; distal scutellar setae 2.
- *Wing* (Fig. 4.30): 6.04mm long and 2.15mm wide; stem vein setose; basicosta dark brown with short hairs and 2 long setae; upper calypter white transparent; lower calypter smoky brown with long black setae, no marginal dark.
- *Halter*: Light brown with brown knob.
- *Fore leg* (Fig. 4.31): Black to brownish; 6.56mm long, coxa 1.13mm long, trochanter 0.55mm long, femur 1.91mm long, tibia 1.70mm long, tarsus 1.27mm long.
- *Abdomen*: 2.23mm long and 3.10mm wide; metallic blue shining with 1st and 2nd tergite black; posterior margins of the 3rd and 4th tergite black banded; presence of setae.
- *Genitalia:* Terminalia round with short setae at the end.
- *Host plant:* unknown.
- *Paratype:* 8 male, 9 female, coll. Divya Jadav. Feb.-Dec., wing and legs on slide, Pinned insects, labeled as above.
- *Distribution:* 3 male, Shirol, 19-II-2014; 4 male, Ajara, 09-XI-2014; 1male, Gaganbawda, 28 -VII-2014; 3 female, Kolhapur, 10-II-2014; 2 female, Shirol, 20-II-2014; 3 female, Ajara, 11-XI-2014; 1 female, Gaganbawda, 28-VII-2014.

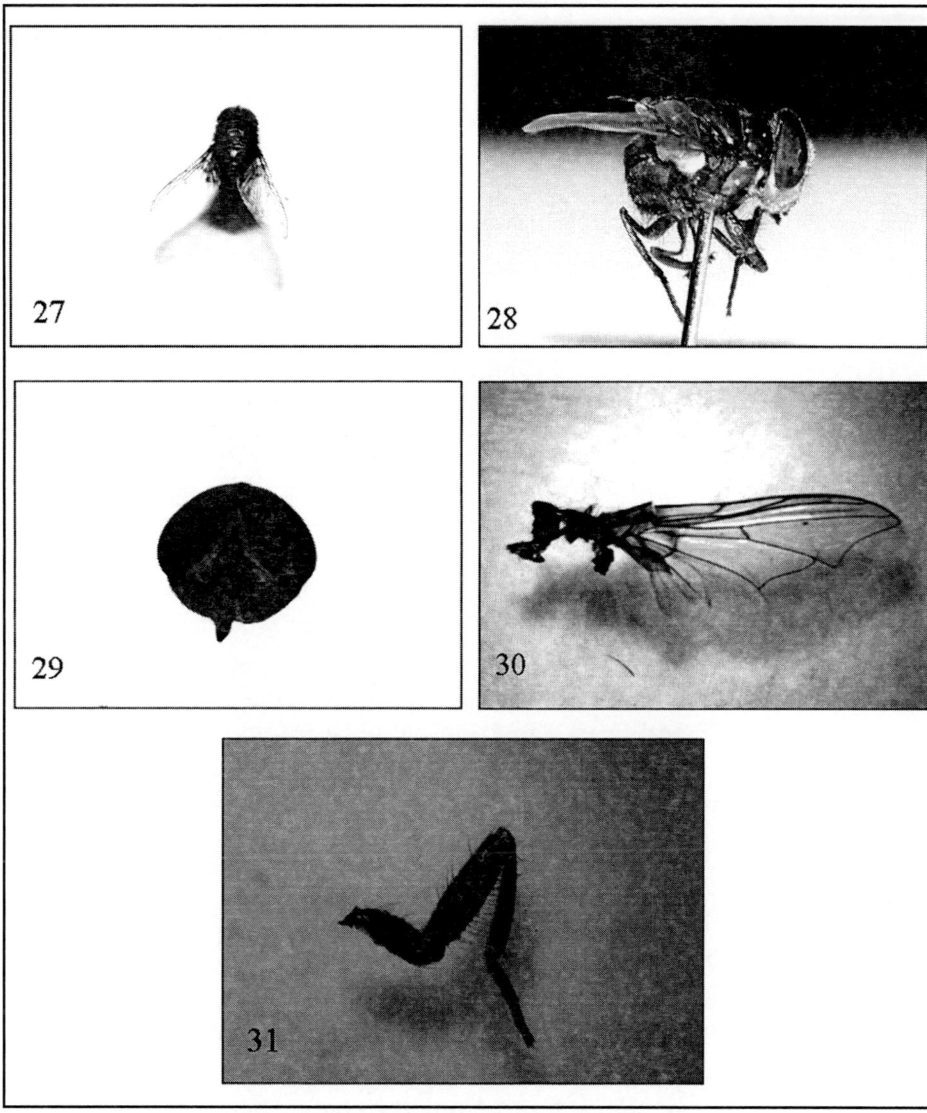

Plate – IV: indica (27-31): Fig. 4.27: **Adult-dorsal view,** Fig. 4.28: **Adult-lateral view,** Fig. 4.29: **Head,** Fig. 4.30: **Wing,** Fig. 4.31: **Fore leg**

Chrysomya megacephala **(Fabricius)**
(Plate - V: Figs. 4.32-4.36)

- *Male* (Fig. 4.32-4.33): Body long 8.35mm, 3.60mm broad; wing 7.82mm long and 3.13mm wide; antenna 1.11mm long, 0.20mm broad; thorax 4.49mm long, 3.35mm broad; abdomen 3.09mm long, 3.10mm broad; foreleg 8.17mm long, black.

- *Head* (Fig. 4.34): 3.22mm long and 4.08mm broad, orange; compound eyes reddish in colour with 2.53mm long and 2.01mm wide; ♂ upper eye facets are enlarged and sharply demarcated from small facets of lower; frontal width 0.01mm; parafrontalia reduced to fine line in ♂, yellow to blackish towards the vertex with black setae; frontal vittae brown; parafacialia and gena yellowish with golden hairs; a pair of fronto orbitals; vibrissa and subvibrissal setule black; palpi yellow with black setae.
- *Antenna*: 1.11mm long, 0.20mm wide; yellow to orange with brownish ends at the tips of first flagellomere; scape black 0.09mm long, 0.18mm wide; pedicel dark orange 0.19mm long, 0.18 mm wide, first flagellomere dark brown 0.83mm long, 0.20mm wide; arista plumose.
- *Flagellar Formula*: S L/W: 0.50, P L/W: 1.05, F L/W: 4.15, A: 1.9.
- *Thorax*: Metallic shining bluish purple; 4.49mm long, 3.35mm broad; prescutum- 1.14mm long, 3.35mm wide, more silvery dusting towards the head than towards scutum with 2 grey stripe; scutum- 1.73mm long, 3.35mm in wide, scutellum- 1.52mm long, 2.24mm in wide; greater ampulla with short black; anterior thoracic spiracle dark brown; proepimeral setae present; acrostical setae 0+1; dorsocentral setae 2+2; intra-alar setae 1; postalar setae 2; supra-alar setae 2; presutural intra alar absent; humeral setae 2; anepisternal setae 3; apical setae 2; subapical setae 2; distal scutellar setae 2.
- *Wing* (Fig. 4.35): 7.28mm in long and 3.13mm in wide; hyaline; stem vein setose; basicosta dark brown with short hairs and 2 long setae; upper calypter white transperant; lower calypter smoky brown with long black setae, margin dark.
- *Halter*: Light brown with brown knob.
- *Fore leg* (Fig. 4.36): Black to brownish; 8.17mm long, coxa 1.26mm long, trochanter 0.58mm long, femur 2.12mm long, setose; tibia 2.11mm long, tarsus 2.10mm long.
- *Abdomen*: 3.09mm long and 3.10mm wide; metallic blue shining with 1st and 2nd tergites black; posterior margins of the 3rd and 4th tergites black banded.
- *Genitalia*: Terminalia round, brown, covered with short golden setae at the end; 1-3 sternites are quadrangular with golden pubescence.
- *Host plant*: unknown.
- *Paratype:* 9 male, 10 female, coll. Divya Jadav. Jan.-Dec, wing and legs on slide, Pinned insects, labelled as above.

- *Distribution:* 2 male, Radhanagari, 10-I-2014; 3 male, Shirol, 23-IX-2014; 1 male, Gaganbawda, 14-XII-2014; 3 male, Kolhapur, 18-XII-2014; 3 female, Radhanagari, 10-I-2014; 2 female, Shirol, 23-IX-2014; 4 male; Gaganbawada, 14-XII-2014; 1 female, Kolhapur, 18-XII-2014.

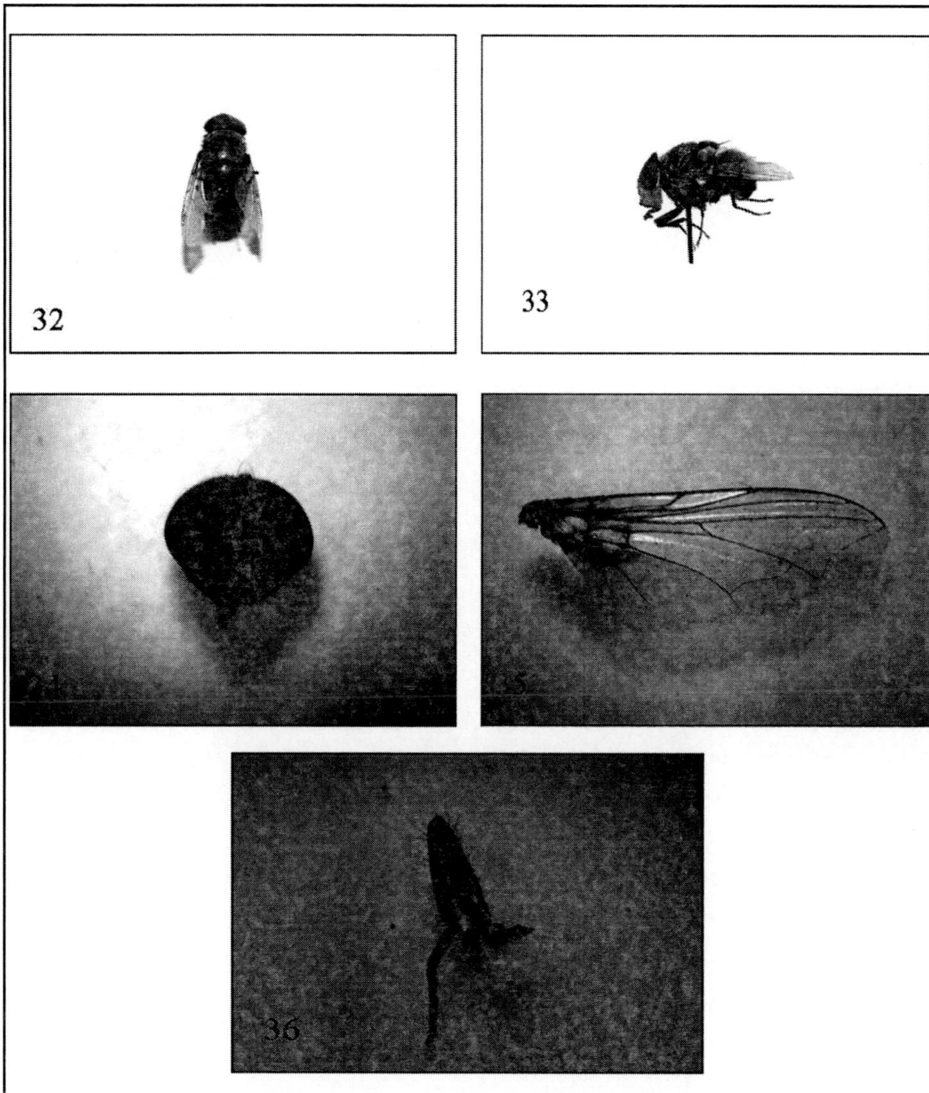

Plate – V *C. megacephala* (32-36): Fig. 4.32: **Adult-dorsal view,** Fig. 4.33: **Adult-lateral view,** Fig. 4.34: **Head,** Fig. 4.35: **Wing,** Fig. 4.36: **Fore leg**

FAMILY SARCOPHAGIDAE

Sarcophagids are flies, dull gray 2.5-18.0 mm long. Thorax usually setae, Abdomen checkered, striped, banded, or spotted; markings usually shifting from brown to black or from dark to pale depending on light incidence.

Subfamily Sarcophaginae

Arista varying from pubeacent to plumose only on basal two-thirds. The oriental species are grayish, the thorax with longitudinal black stripes, the abdomen either with a grey and black tesselate pattern which varies with the light incidence, or with fixed black markings on a grey ground. Wing with stem-vein setulose on posterior upper side of its basal section. The two anterior bristles on the area between the presuturals dorso-centrals and the notopleurals are either in a longitudinal line or the anterior one is situated nearer the mid-line than the posterior.

Key to the Genera of subfamily Sarcophaginae (Senior- White *et al.* 1940)

1. Abdominal markings variable with light incidence .... 2.
   – Abdominal markings fixed in position .... 3.
2. Arista plumose on basal two-thirds. sternopleurals 1:1:1 or 1:1 *Sarcophaga Mg.*
   – Arista pubescent. Sternopleurals 1:1 .... *Sarcophila* Rond.
3. ♂ without external fronto-orbitals. Sternoplurals 1:1 .... *Agria* Macq
   – ♂ with external fronto-orbitals. Sternoplurals 2:1 .... *Wohlfartia* B.&B.

Sarcophaga Meigen 1826

It contain small to large flies with grey colour and dorso central black thoracic stripes, grey and black tessellate pattern on the abdomen. From India 17 species have been reported.

Key to Species of Genus *Sarcophaga* Meigen 1826

1. Posterio dorsocentral setae 3 2
   – Posterio dorsocentral setae 4 15
2. Acrostichal setae only present as prescutellar setae 3
   – Acrostichal setae also present prescutellar setae 3
3. Segment iii of costa shorter than v; vein I bristly .... *calicifera* bott.
   – Segment iii of costa equal or longer than v; vein I bare 4
4. Frons less than half of eye 5
   – Frons greater than half of eye 7
5. Hind tibia bare .... *caudagalli* bott.
   – Hind tibia hairy and fringed 6
6. Second abdominal segment with marginal setae 7
   – Second abdominal segment without marginal setae ....*josephi* bott.

7. Preputium trilobite ....*pea - helicis* Sen.
   – Lateral apophysis elongate, filiform .... *sera* Rohd.
8. Genae and genital segment 2 black .... *melanura* Mg.
   – Genae white, genital segment 2 reddish .... *barbata* Thom.
9. Frons narrow 10
   – Frons varying in length 11
10. Wings basally deep yellow .... *basalis* Wlk.
   – Wings slightly infuscated .... *gravelyi* Sen.
11. Frons broad .... *heamatodes* Mg.
   – Frons not exceeding half as eye width 12
12. Superior claspers smooth and hairy 13
   – Superior claspers laterally spinulose 14
13. Accessory forceps normal .... *valangx* Aldr.
   – Accessory forceps not spinulose in fork .... *aspinata* Sen.
14. Superior clasper spinulose .... *kastneri* Baran.
   – Superior clasper spinulose on apical half .... *baranoffi* sen and whit.
15. Prescutellar acrostichal setae absent 16
   – Prescutellar acrostichal setae present 17
16. Coloration normal .... *walayari* Sen
   – Hinder abdominal segments bright golden .... *doleschalli* J.&T.
17. Presutural acrostichal setae present 18
   – Presutural acrostichal setae absent 31
18. Presutural acrostichal setae 4 to 5 19
   – Presutural acrostichal setae 1 24
19. Elongated species face silvery 20
   – Shape normal face golden 22
20. Superior claspers spinulose 21
   – Superior claspers bare .... *banski* Sen. Wh.
21. Accessory forceps V shaped .... *henryi* Sen. Wh.
   – Accessory forceps inwardly projecting 22
22. Anepisternal setae 5 .... *pusana* Sen. Wh.
   – Anepisternal setae 6 .... *udagiriensis* sp. nov.
23. Superior claspers with marginal setae 24
   – Superior claspers separated strong setae 25

24. Superior claspers with separate strong setae .... *antilope* Bott.
    – Superior claspers with set of setae .... *ostindiex* Sen. Wh.
25. Face golden .... *basiseta* Baran
    – Face yellowish .... *kankauensis* Baran
26. Mid tibia fringed .... *annandalei* Sen. Wh.
    – Mid tibia bare 27
27. Frons and face bright golden 28
    – Frons and face yellowish grey 29
28. With golden body .... *prosbaliina* Baran.
    – Without golden body .... *knabi* Parker
29. Palpi black .... *albiceps* Mg.
    – Palpi yellow 30
30. Mid tibia fringed .... *phaenicopterus* Bott.
    – Mid tibia bare 31
31. Genital segment 2 red .... *hirtipes* Wd.
    – Genital segment 2 black .... *hirtipes* var. orchidea.
32. Third antennal segment four times second 33
    – Third antennal segment two and half times second 37
33. Hind tibia bare .... *talonata* Sen. Wh.
    – Hind tibia hairy 34
34. Mid tibia fringed .... *krameri* Bott.
    – Mid tibia fringed 35
35. Frons broader .... *beesoni* Sen. Wh.
    – Frons narrower 36
36. Genital segment 2 red .... *pattoni* Sen. Wh.
    – Genital segment 2 black .... *formosana* Sen Wh.
37. Mid tibia hairy, fringed .... *orientalis* Park.
    – Mid tibia bare .... *crinita* Park.

Sarcophaga josephi Buttcher
(Plate - VI: Figs. 4.37-4.41)

- *Male* (Fig. 4.37-4.38): Body long 11.77mm, wide 4.15mm; wing 10.93mm long and 4.14mm wide; antenna 1.55mm long, 0.42mm broad; thorax 7.04mm long, 3.36mm broad with three black stripes; hind leg 10.55mm long, black; abdomen 6.30mm long, 4.14mm broad with black and grey patches.

- *Head* (Fig.4.39): 3.05mm long, 3.77 mm broad; reddish brown eyes, eyefacets are small and uniform, 2.62mm long, 1.52mm wide; presence of 2 ocellar setae; frontal wide 0.73mm; fronto orbital plate brown and narrow towards vertex; presence of 6-7 frontal setae; presence of 1 reclinate orbital setae; parafacial covered with silvery microtomentum with single row of setae along the eye margin; frontal vitta dark brown; face silvery with light brown lower edge; genal dilation and gena silvery with pale white setae; vibrissa and subvibrissal setule black; palpi brown.
- *Antenna*: 1.55mm long; scape black- 0.03mm long, 0.04mm wide, pedicel dark brown 0.42mm long, 0.22mm wide, frist flagellomere dark brown- 1.10mm long, 0.42mm wide; arista plumose.
- *Flagellar Formula*: S L/W: 0.75, P L/W: 1.9, F L/W: 2.61, A: 1.76.
- *Thorax*: 7.04mm long, prescutum- 2.01mm long, 3.36mm wide, scutem- 3.35mm long, mm in wide, scutellum- 1.68mm long, 2.13mm wide usually three black stripe; anterior spiracle dull white; proepimeral setae present; acrostical setae 0+2; dorsocentral setae 0+2; intra-alar setae 1+2; postalar setae 2; supraalar setae 3; postpronotal/humeral setae 3; notoplueral setae only 2 primaries + 2 subprimaries; anepisternal setae 5; katepisternal setae 2+1; meroplueral setae 11; postalar wall setose; apical setae 2; subapical setae 2; absence of distal scutellar setae; coxoplueral streak absent.
- *Wing* (Fig. 4.40): 10.93 mm long and 4.15mm wide; tegula pale white; basicosta pale with black setae; r_{4+5} vein setose; costal spine absent; no subcoastal break; upper and lower calypter whitish and bare expect pale minute hairs at the margin.
- *Halter:* Dark brown with light brown knob.
- *Leg:* Brown colour; fore, mid and hind coxa densely hairy; mid and hind tibia are also hairy at their ends; foreleg 9.77mm long, coxa 0.80mm long, trochanter 0.96mm long, femur 3.20mm long, tibia 2.66mm long, tarsus 2.15mm long; midleg: 9.35mm long, coxa 0.85mm long, trochanter 0.95mm long, femur 3.13mm long, tibia 2.32mm long, tarsus 2.10mm long.
- *Hind leg* (Fig.4.41): 10.55mm long, coxa 1.20mm long, trochanter 0.85mm long, femur 3.01mm long, tibia 3.00mm long, tarsus 2.49mm long.
- *Abdomen*: 6.30mm long and 4.41 mm wide; abdomen with long median stripe which extends from 3rd tergite to 5th tergites; on either sides of median stripe there are elongated grey patches; presence of marginal setae at the posterior margins of the 4th and 5th tergite; 1-3 sternites are quadrangular.
- *Genitalia:* Terminalia round, light brown, pear shaped setose; 1-3 Sternite are quadrangular.
- *Host plant:* unknown.

- *Paratype:* 3 male, 2 female, coll. Divya Jadav. Throughout the year, wing and legs on slide, Pinned insects, labeled as above.
- *Distribution:* 1 male, Radhanagari, 10-I-2014; 1 male, Shirol, 23-IX-2014; 1male, Gaganbawda, 14-XII-2014; 2 male, Kolhapur, 18-XII-2014;3 female, Radhanagari, 10-I-2014; 1 female, Gaganbavda, 14-XII-2014; 1 female, Kolhapur, 18-XII-2014.

Plate – VI *S. josephi* (37-41): Fig. 4.37: **Adult-dorsal view,** Fig. 4.38: **Adult-lateral view,** Fig. 4.39: **Head,** Fig. 4.40: **Wing,** Fig. 4.41: **Hind leg**

Sarcophaga Pes-helicis Senior-White
(Plate - VII: Figs. 4.42-4.45)

- *Male* (Fig. 4.42-4.43): Body long 9.76mm, wide 2.75mm; wing 7.03mm long and 3.12mm wide; antenna 1.47mm long, 0.88mm wide; thorax 4.05mm long, 2.56mm broad with three black stripes; hind leg 7.83mm long, black; abdomen 6.35mm long, 2.96mm broad with black and grey patches.
- *Head* (Fig. 4.44): 2.34mm long and 2.75mm broad, greyish black; compound eyes reddish brown in colour with 1.62mm long and 0.92mm wide; presence of 2 ocellar setae; three clear row of black post ocular cilia; frontal wide 0.91mm, about half an eye wide; fronto orbital covered with silvery microtomentum with very few black patches; presence of 8 frontal setae; presence of 1 proclinate orbital setae; parafacial covered with silvery microtomentum with single row of setae along the eye margin; forntal vittae dark brown and blackish towards vertex; face silvery with light brown lower edge; genal dilation and gena covered with silvery microtomentum and pale white setae except at genal dilations near facial ridges which has very few black setae; vibrissa and subvibrissal setule black; palpi dark brown.
- *Antenna*: 1.47mm long, 0.88mm wide; scape black 0.22mm long, 0.88mm wide; pedicel dark brown 0.25mm long, 0.05mm wide; frist flagellomere grayish black 0.67mm long, 0.25mm wide; arista plumose.
- *Flagellar Formula*: S L/W: 0.0025, P L/W:5 , F L/W: 2.68, A: 2.56.
- *Thorax*: 4.05mm long, 2.56mm broad; prescutum 1.31mm long, 2.56mm wide; scutum- 1.65mm long, 2.43mm wide; scutellum 1.09mm long, 1.70mm wide; usually three black stripe; anterior spriracle light brown; proepimeral setae present; acrostical setae 2+2; dorsocentral setae 3+3; intra-alar setae 1+2; postalar setae 2; postpronotal/humeral setae 3; notoplueral setae 2primaries+2 subprimaries; katepisternal setae 6; meroplueral setae 8; postalar wall 3 short setae; apical setae 2; subapical setae 2; distal scutellar setae 2; coxoplueral streak present.
- *Wing* (Fig. 4.45): 7.03mm long, 3.12mm wide; tegula pale white; basicosta pale with black setae; R_{4+5} vein setose; costal spine absent; no subcoastal break; upper and lower calypter whitish and bare expect pale minute hairs at the margin.

  Halter dark brown with light brown knob.
- *Leg*: Black; foreleg: 8.20mm long, coxa 0.84mm long, trochanter 0.54mm long, femur 2.49mm long, tibia 2.12mm long, tarsus 2.21mm long; midleg: 5.81mm long, coxa 0.48mm long, trochanter 0.40mm long, femur 1.80mm long, tibia 1.49mm long, tarsus 1.64mm long; hind leg: 7.83mm long coxa 0.85mm long, trochanter 0.59mm long, femur 2.55mm long, tibia 1.98mm long, tarsus 1.86mm long.

- *Abdomen*: 4.41mm long and 2.66 mm wide; abdomen with elongate and triangular black patches along median stripe which is darker at 3rd tergite and light brown at 4th and 5th tergites; on 3rd tergite it is elongated patch, 4th it is triangular and quadrangular at the 5th tergite; 4th tergite has marginal setae at the posterior margins of the segment; posterior margins of the 5th tergite thickly setose.
- *Genitalia*: Terminalia round, black, densely covered with short setae at the end; 1-3 sternites are quadrangular and reducing in size towards terminalia.
- *Host plant:* unknown.
- *Paratype:* 10 male, 6 female, coll. Divya Jadav. May-Oct., wing and legs on slide, pinned insects, labelled as above.
- *Distribution:* 1 male, Radhanagari, 10-V-2014; 3 male, Shirol, 23-V-2014; 2 male, Gaganbawda, 14-X-2014; 4 male, Kolhapur, 18-XII-2014; 2 female, Radhanagari, 10-V-2014; 4 female, Shirol, 23-V-2014.

Plate – VII *S. pes-helicis* (42-45): Fig. 4.42: **Adult-dorsal view,** Fig. 4.43: **Adult-lateral view,** Fig. 4.44: **Head,** Fig. 4.45: **Wing**

Sarcophaga sera Rohd.

(Plate - VIII: Figs. 4.46-4.50) (See Page no. 53)

- *Male* (Fig. 4.46-4.47): Body long 12.36mm, wide 2.96mm; wing 9.72mm long and 3.42mm wide; antenna 0.99mm long; thorax 5.05mm long, 2.96mm broad with three black stripes; hind leg 11.68mm long, black; abdomen 6.35mm long, 2.96mm broad with black and grey patches.
- *Head* (Fig. 4.48): 2.09mm long and 2.29mm broad, grayish black; compound eyes reddish brown in colour with 1.65mm long and 1.06mm wide; frontal wide 0.56mm; presence of 2 ocellar setae; fronto orbital covered with silvery microtomentum and narrow towards vertex; presence of 7-8 frontal setae; presence of 1 proclinate orbital setae; parafacial covered with silvery microtomentum with single row of setae along the eye margin; forntal vittae dark brown and blackish towards vertex; face silvery with light brown lower edge; genal dilation and gena covered with silvery with pale white setae; vibrissa and subvibrissal setule black; palpi black.
- *Antenna*: Aristate type; 0.99mm long, 0.20mm broad; Scape black 0.04mm long and 0.01mm wide; Pedicel dark brown 0.41mm long and 0.19mm in wide; First Flagellomere grayish black 0.55mm long and 0.20mm in wide; arista plumose.
- *Flagellar Formula*: S L/W: 4, P L/W: 2.15, F L/W: 2.75, A: 2.97.
- *Thorax*: 5.05mm long, 2.96mm broad; prescutum- 1.53mm long, 2.70mm broad; scutum- 2.23mm long, 2.96mm in broad; scutellum- 1.29mm long, 2.06mm broad; usually three black stripe; anterior spiracle light brown; proepimeral setae present; acrostical setae 2+2; dorsocentral setae 4+4; intra-alar setae 1+2; postalar setae 2; supraalar setae 3; postpronotal/ humeral setae 3; notoplueral setae only 2 primaries; anepisternal setae 3; katepisternal setae 1+1; meroplueral setae 10; postalar wall 3 short setae; apical setae 2; subapical setae 2; distal scutellar setae 2; coxoplueral streak present.
- *Wing* (Fig. 4.49): 9.72mm long, 3.42mm in broad; Tegula pale white; Basicosta pale with black setae; R_{4+5} veinsetose; Costal spine absent; No subcoastal break; Upper and lower calypter whitish and bare expect pale minute hairs at the margin.
- *Halter*: Dark brown with light brown knob.
- *Legs:* Black except at mid and hind trochanter, which is light brown; the mid and hind tibia with dense long black hairs; foreleg: 10.57mm long, coxa 0.71mm long, trochanter 0.43mm long, femur 3.68mm long, tibia 3.08mm long, tarsus 2.67mm long; midleg: 11.53mm long, coxa 0.86mm long, trochanter 0.68mm long, femur 3.83mm long, tibia 3.48mm long, tarsus 2.68mm long.

- *Hind leg* (Fig. 4.50): 11.74mm long, coxa 1.09mm long, trochanter 0.69mm long, femur 3.61mm long, tibia 3.66mm long, tarsus 2.69mm long.
- *Abdomen:* 6.35mm long and 2.96 mm wide; abdomen with long median stripe which extends from 3rd tergite to 5th tergites.on either sides of median stripe there are elongated black patches on 3rd tergite and bronze with dark margin patches on the 4th and 5th tergite; presence of marginal setae at the posterior margins of the 4th and 5th tergite; posterior margins of the 5th tergite thickly setose; 1-3 sternites are quadrangular.
- *Genitalia:* Terminalia round, light brown, densely covered with short setae at the end.
- *Host plant:* unknown.
- *Paratype:* 6 male, 4 female, coll. Divya jadav. Feb.-April, wing and legs on slide, Pinned insects, labeled as above.
- *Distribution:* 1 male, Gaganbawda, 26-II-2014; 2 male, Shirol, 04-II-2014; 3 male Radhanagari, 25-IX-2014;3 female, Gaganbawda, 26-II-2014; 1 female, Shirol, 04-II-2014.

Sarcophaga baranoffi Senior-White
(Plate - IX: Figs. 4.51-4.55)

- *Male* (Fig. 4.51-4.52): Body long 9.5mm, wide 2.77mm; wing 6.98mm long and 2.68mm wide; antenna 0.89mm long, 0.22mm wide; thorax 3.49mm long, 2.09mm broad with three black stripes; hind leg 8.84mm long, black; abdomen mm long, mm broad with black and grey patches.
- *Head* (Fig. 53): 1.92mm long and 2.77mm broad, creamy brown; compound eyes reddish brown in colour with 1.48mm long and 1.01mm wide; frontal wide 0.75mm; frons not exceeding to fifth an eye; dark brown; presence of 2 ocellar setae; fronto orbital and parafacial plates were dusty brown. fronto orbital plate narrow towards vertex; presence of 7-8 frontal setae; presence of 1 reclinate orbital setae; parafacial plate with single row of setae along the eye margin; forntal vittae dark brown and blackish towards vertex; face light brown; genal dilation creamy brown and gena bluish black with pale white setae; vibrissa and subvibrissal setule black; palpi black; orbit and occiput bluish.
- *Antenna*: 0.89mm long, 0.22mm wide; scape black- 0.09mm long, 0.03mm wide, pedicel black- 0.24mm long, 0.22mm wide, first flagellomere creamy brown- 0.56mm long, 0.22mm wide; arista plumose.
- *Flagellar Formula*: S L/W: 3, P L/W: 1.09, F L/W: 2.55, Average: 2.21.

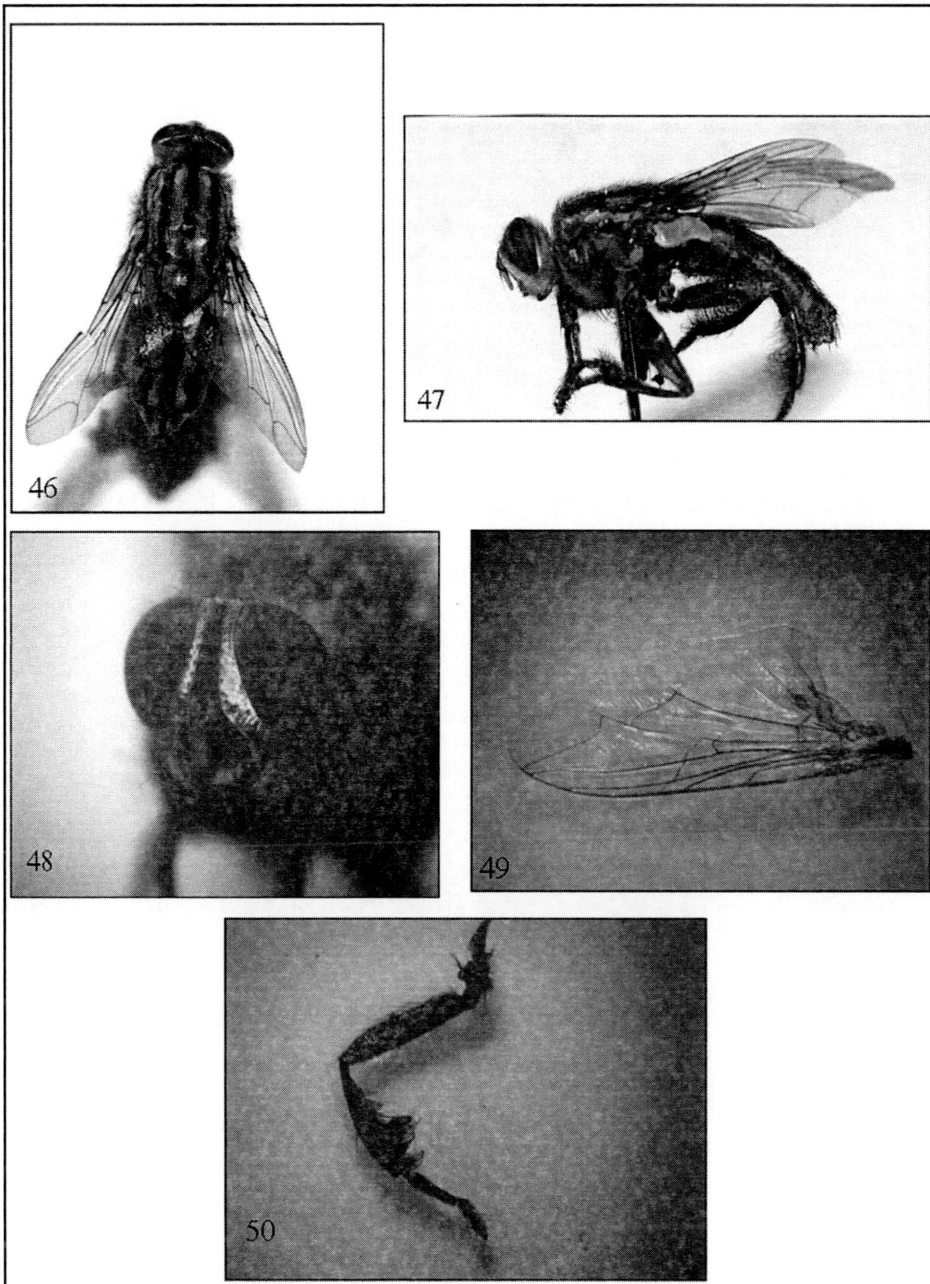

Plate – VIII *S. sera* (46-50): Fig. 4.46: **Adult-dorsal view,** Fig. 4.47: **Adult-lateral view,** Fig. 4.48: **Head,** Fig. 4.49: **Wing,** Fig. 4.50 **Hind leg**

- *Thorax*: 3.49mm long, 2.09mm broad; prescutum- 1.09mm long, 2.09mm wide; scutum- 1.55mm long, 2.08mm wide; scutellum- 0.85mm long, 1.44mm wide; usually three black stripe; anterior spiracle light brown; proepimeral setae present; acrostical setae 2+2; dorsocentral setae 3+3; intra-alar setae 1; postalar setae 2; supraalar setae 3; postpronotal/ humeral setae 3; notoplueral setae only 2 primaries + 2 subprimaries; anepisternal setae 6; katepisternal setae 2+1; meroplueral setae 10; postalar wall bare; apical setae 2; subapical setae 2; distal scutellar setae 2; coxoplueral streak absent.
- *Wing* (Fig. 4.54): 6.98mm long and 2.68mm wide; brown; tegula pale white; basicosta pale with black setae; r_{4+5} vein setose; costal spine absent; no subcoastal break; upper and lower calypter whitish and bare expect pale minute hairs at the margin.
- *Halter*: Dark brown with light brown knob.
- *Leg*: Fore femur covered with grey to mentum; hind femur with grey reflections, other parts are brown in colour; fore leg: 7.33mm long; coxa 0.91mm long, trochanter 0.62mm long, femur 2.31mm long, tibia 1.67mm long, tarsus 1.82mm long; mid leg: 8.12mm long; coxa 0.79mm long, trochanter 0.57mm long, femur 2.34mm long, with fine bristles entirely; tibia 2.11mm long, tarsus 2.31mm long.
- *Hind leg* (Fig. 4.55): 8.84mm long; coxa 0.72mm long, trochanter 0.72mm long, femur 2.11mm long, tibia 2.49mm long with 2 bristles on front and hind side, tarsus 2.80mm long.
- *Abdomen*: 4.55mm long and 2.53 mm wide; abdomen with well-marked bends and long median stripe which extends from 3rd tergite to 5th tergites on either sides of median stripe triangular grey patches on 3rd tergite and black and grey patches on the 4th and 5th tergite; presence of marginal setae at the posterior margins of the 4th and 5th tergite.
- *Genitalia*: Terminalia round, black and covered with short setae at the end. 1-3 sternites are quadrangular.
- *Host plant:* unknown.
- *Paratype:* 7 male, 6 female, coll. Divya Jadav. Feb.-May, wing and legs on slide, Pinned insects, labelled as above.
- *Distribution:* 2 male, Radhanagari, 10-I-2014; 1male, Shirol, 23-IX-2014; 2 male, Gaganbavda, 14-XII-2014; 2 male, Kolhapur, 18-XII-2014;2 female, Radhanagari, 10-I-2014; 2 female, Gaganbavda, 14-XII-2014; 2 female, Kolhapur, 18-XII-2014.

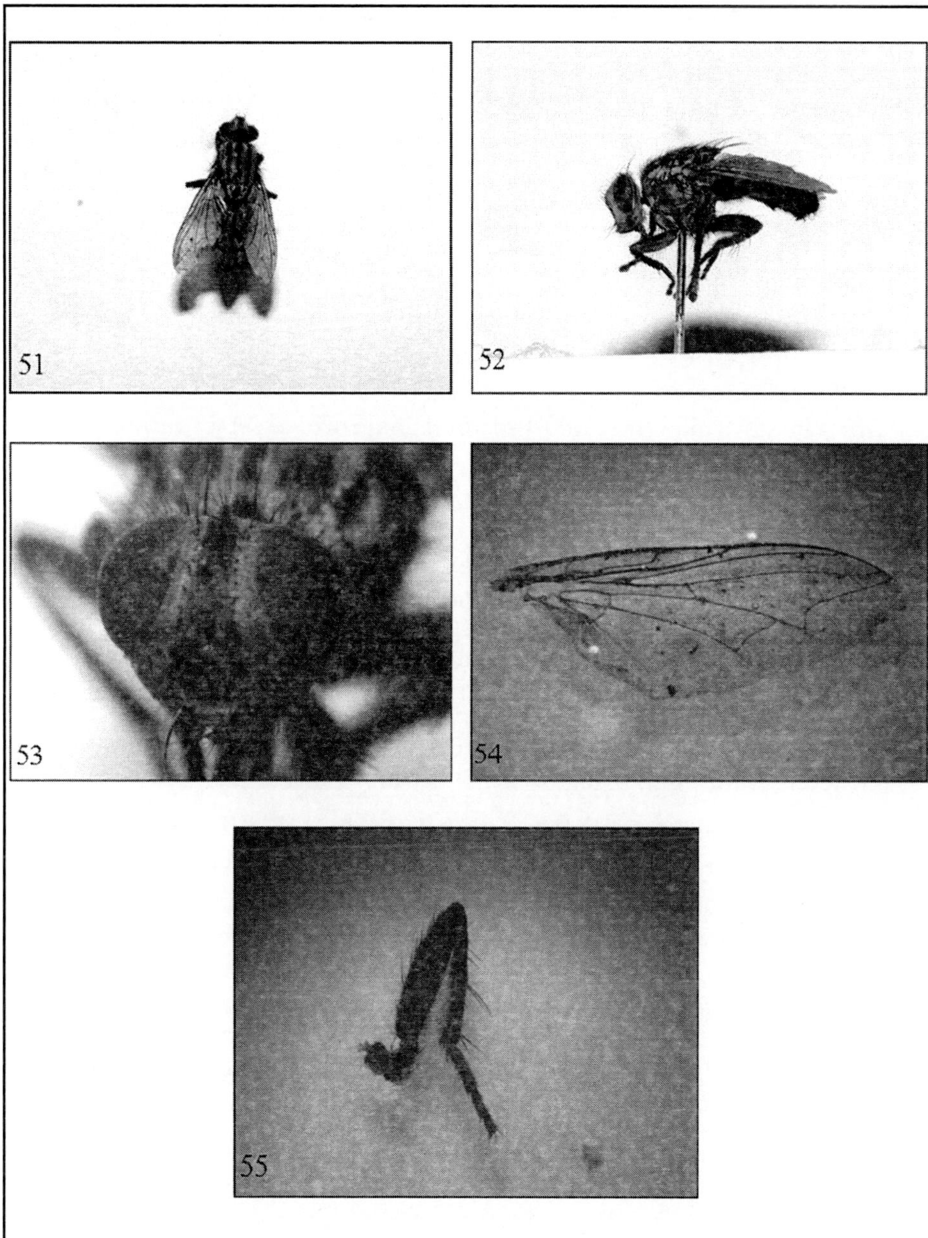

Plate – IX *S. baranoffi* (51-55): Fig. 4.51: **Adult-dorsal view,** Fig. 4.52: **Adult-lateral view,** Fig. 4.53: **Head,** Fig. 4.54: **Wing,** Fig. 4.55: **Hind leg**

Sarcophaga pusana **Senior-White**

(Plate - X: Figs. 4.56-4.62) (See page no. 58)

- *Male* (Fig. 4.56-4.57): Body long 11.77mm, wide 4.15mm; wing 9.37mm long and 3.20mm wide; antenna 1.15mm long, 0.35mm wide; thorax 5.18mm long, 3.42mm wide with three black stripes; hind leg 8.47mm long, black; abdomen 5.20mm long, 4.14mm wide with black and grey patches.
- *Head* (Fig. 4.58): 2.71mm long and 4.11mm broad, greyish black; compound eyes reddish brown in colour with 1.86mm long and 1.35mm wide; frontal wide 1.41mm, 2.5 times of eye; presence of 2 ocellar setae; fronto orbital plate broad, covered with silvery microtomentum and are blackish towards vertex; presence of 10-11 frontal setae; presence of 2 proclinate orbital setae and 1 rectinoclinate orbital setae; parafacialplate black, covered with grey microtomentum with single row of setae along the eye margin; forntal vittae dark brown to blackish towards vertex with a row of 5-6 setalue along its external margin reaching the level of ocellar triangle; face silvery till the edge, strong not golden but silvery; genal dilation creamy with few black setae near the facial ridge and gena grey covered with pale white hairs; vibrissa and subvibrissal setule black; palpi black; 3 rows of irregular black post ocular setae.
- *Antenna*: Antenna 1.15mm long, scape black 0.09mm long, 0.15mm wide; pedicel dark brown 0.24mm long, 0.21mm wide, first flagellomere dark brown0.82mm long, 0.35mm wide; arista plumose.
- *Flagellar Formula*: S L/W: 0.6, P L/W: 1.14, F L/W: 2.34, A: 1.36.
- *Thorax*: Whitish grey; 5.18mm long, prescutum- 1.39mm long, 3.10m wide, scutum- 2.61mm long, 3.42mm wide, scutellum- 1.18mm long, 2.10mm wide; usually three black stripe; anterior spiracle light brown; proepimeral setae present; acrostical setae 5+1; dorsocentral setae 4+4; intra-alar setae 1+2; postalar setae 2; supraalar setae 3; prescutellar acrosticals absent; presutural acrosticals present, only one presutural acrosticals present; postpronotal/humeral setae 3; propluron bare and black; notoplueral setae only 2primaries and 2subprimaries; anepisternal setae 6; katepisternal setae 2+1; meroplueral setae 8-9 postalar wall-presence of setae in middle; apical setae 2; subapical setae 2; distal scutellar setae 2; coxoplueral streak absent.
- *Wing* (Fig. 4.59): 9.37mm in long and 3.20mm in wide; tegula pale white; basicosta pale with black setae; r_{4+5} vein setose; costal spine absent; no subcoastal break; upper and lower calypter whitish and bare expect pale minute hairs at the margin.

- *Halter*: Dark brown with light brown knob.
- *Leg*: Black; fore leg: 8.45mm long, coxa 1.30mm long, trochanter 0.47mm long, femur 2.22mm long, tibia 2.20 mm long, tarsus 2.26mm long; midleg: 7.73mm long, coxa 0.42mm long, trochanter 0.36mm long, femur 2.56mm long, tibia 2.96 mm long, tarsus 1.43mm long.
- *Hind leg* (Fig. 4.62): 8.47mm long, coxa 0.67mm long, trochanter 0.28mm long, femur 3.00mm long, tibia 2.68mm long, fringed; tarsus 1.84mm long.
- *Abdomen* (Fig. 4.60-4.61): 5.20mm long and 4.14mm wide; abdominal markings variable with light incidence; second tergite of abdomen bare; abdomen withlong median stripe which extends from 3rd tergite to 5th tergites on either sides of median stripe there are triangular grey patches from 3rd tergite to 5th tergites; presence of marginal setae at the posterior margins of the 4th and 5th tergite.
- *Genitalia:* Terminalia round, orange, densely covered with short setae at the end; 1-3 sternites are quadrangular.
- *Host plant:* unknown.
- *Paratype:* 2 male, 1 female, coll. Divya Jadav. Jan-May, wing and legs on slide, Pinned insects, labelled as above.
- *Distribution:* 1 male, Gaganbawda, 26-II-2014; 1 male, Shirol, 04-II-2014; 1 male Radhanagari, 25-V-2014; 3 female, Gaganbawda, 26-II-2014; 1 female, Shirol, 04-II-2014.

***Sarcophaga udhagiriensis* sp. nov.**

(Plate - XI: Figs. 4.63-4.68)

- *Male* (Fig. 4.63-4.64): Body 12.69mm long, 3.46mm broad; wing 9.28mm long and 3.97mm wide; antenna 1.75mm long; thorax 5.64mm long, 3.46mm broad with three black stripes; hind leg 8.61mm long, black; abdomen 5.70mm long, 3.23mm broad with black and grey patches.
- *Head* (Fig. 4.65): 2.59mm long, 3.46mm broad; grayish black; compound eyes reddish brown in colour with 1.99mm long and 1.17mm wide; frontal wide 1.12mm; presence of 2 ocellar setae; fronto-orbital and parafacial plates covered with silvery grey microtomentum: fronto - orbital plates broader at the vertex; presence of 8-9 frontal setae; presence of 2 proclinate and 1 rectinoclinate orbital setae; parafacial covered with silvery microtomentum with single row of setae along the eye margin; forntal vittae dark black; face and its edge silvery; genal dilation and gena silvery with pale white setae except near facial ridge few black setae are scattered; vibrissa and subvibrissal setule black; palpi black.
- *Antenna*: Antenna 1.75mm long and 0.26mm broad; scape black, 0.7mm long, 0.12mm broad; pedicel dark brown, 0.14mm long, 0.26mm broad; first flagellomere dark brown, 0.91mm long, 0.14mm broad; arista plumose.

Plate – X *S. pusana* (56-62): Fig. 4.56: **Adult-dorsal view,** Fig. 4.57: **Adult-lateral view,** Fig. 4.58: **Head,** Fig. 4.59: **Wing,** Fig. 4.60: **Abdomen dorsal view,** Fig. 4.61: **Abdomen ventral view,** Fig.4.62: **Hind leg**

- *Flagellar Formula:* S L/W: 5.83, P L/W: 0.54, F L/W: 6.5, Average: 4.29.
- *Thorax*: 5.64mm long, 3.46mm broad; prothorax 2.03mm long, 3.46mm in broad; mesothorax 2.16mm long, 3.22mm in wide; metathorax 1.45mm long, 1.85mmin wide, usually three black stripe; anterior spiracle light brown; proepimeral setae present; acrostical setae 2+2; dorsocentral setae 4+4; intra-alar setae 1+2; postalar setae 2; supraalar setae 3; postpronotal/ humeral setae 3; notoplueral setae only 2 primaries and 2 subprimaries; anepisternal setae 5; katepisternal setae 1+2; meroplueral setae 9; postalar wall bare; apical setae 2; subapical setae 2; distal scutellar setae 2; coxoplueral streak present.
- *Wing* (Fig. 4.66): 9.28mm in long and 3.97mm in broad; tegula pale white; basicosta pale with black setae; r_{4+5} vein setose; costal spine absent; no subcoastal break; upper and lower calypter whitish and bare expect pale minute hairs at the margin.
- *Halter*: Dark brown with light brown knob.
- *Leg*: Black; fore leg: 9.22mm long, coxa 1.25mm long, trochanter 0.54mm long, femur 2.76mm long, tibia 2.23mm long, tarsus 2.44mm long; mid leg: 9.09mm long, coxa 1.23mm long, trochanter 0.64mm long, femur 2.93mm long, tibia 2.55mm long, tarsus 1.74mm long.
- *Hind leg* (Fig. 4.68): 8.61mm long, coxa 1.07mm long, trochanter 0.79mm, long; femur 2.69mm long, tibia 3.01mm long, tarsus 1.05mm long.
- *Abdomen* (Fig. 4.67): Abdomen 5.70mm long and 3.23mm wide; abdomen with long median stripe which extends from 3rd tergite to 5th tergites, on either sides of median stripe there are gray patches on 3-4 tergite while dark patch on 5th tergite; 4th tergite; posterior margins of the 4th and 5th tergitese tose.
- *Genitalia*: Terminalia round, light brown, densely covered with short setae at the end; 1-3 sternites are irregular in shape.

REMARKS

This species runs close to *Sarcophaga pusana* Senior-White by having:

1. Palpi black.
2. Antennal scape black.
3. Prescutellar acrostichals absent.

However, it differs from above species by:

1. Body proportion *i.e.* 12.69mm X 3.46mm.
2. Flagellar Formula: S L/W: 5.83, P L/W: 0.54, F L/W: 6.5, Average: 4.29.
3. Presence of 8-9 frontal setae.
4. Anepisternal setae 5.

- *Host plant:* unknown.
- *Holotype:* 1 male, coll. Divya Jadav. Feb.-May, wing and legs on slide, pinned insects, labeled as above.
- *Etymology*: The specimen was collected from *Udhagiri* region of Maharashtra, India so *Udhagiriensis* species is given.
- *Distribution:* 1 male, Gaganbawda, 10-III-2014.

Plate – XI *S.udagiriensis* (63-68): Fig. 4.63: **Adult-dorsal view,** Fig. 4.64: **Adult-lateral view,** Fig. 4.65: **Head,** Fig. 4.66: **Wing,** Fig. 4.67: **Abdomen ventral view,** Fig. 4.68: **Hind leg**

***Sarcophaga orientalis* Parker**
(Plate - XII: Figs. 4.69-4.74)

- *Male* (Fig. 4.69-4.70): Body long 8.82mm, wide 3.20mm; wing 5.97mm long and 3.02mm wide; antenna 1.03mm long; thorax 3.54mm long, 2.41mm broad with three black stripes; hind leg 7.46mm long, black; abdomen 4.50mm long, 2.39mm broad with black and grey patches.
- *Head* (Fig. 4.71): 2.14mm long and 3.20mm broad, grayish; compound eyes reddish brown in colour with 1.51mm long and 1.20mm wide; frontal wide 0.80mm; presence of 2 ocellar setae; fronto orbital plate narrow towards vertex and blackish and covered with light brown microtomentum towards parafacial plate; presence of 7-8 frontal setae; presence of 1 reclinate orbital setae only; parafacial plate black with spotted silvery microtomentum with single row of very weak setae along the eye margin; forntal vittae black with a row of 3-4 setule along its external margin near the upper half; face silvery with light brown lower edge; genal dilation silvery with black seta; gena black with black hairs; vibrissa and subvibrissal setule black; palpi black.
- *Antenna*: 1.03mm long and 0.19mm broad; scape black- 0.06mm long, 0.03mm wide; pedicel black- 0.30mm long, 0.19mm wide, first flagellomere dark brown- 0.67mm long, 0.30mm wide; arista plumose.
- *Flagellar Formula*: S L/W: 2, P L/W: 1.57 , F L/W: 2.23, A: 1.93.
- *Thorax*: 3.54mm in long, 2.34mm broad; greyish yellow; prescutem 1.17mm long, 2.34mm wide; scutem 1.41 mm long, 2.41 wide; scutellum 0.96mm long, 1.33mm wide; usually three black stripe; anterior spiracle light brown; proepimeral setae present; acrostical setae 0+2; dorsocentral setae 4+4; intra-alar setae 1+2; postalar setae 2; postpronotal/humeral setae 3; notoplueral setae 2 primaries + 2 subprimaries; anepisternal bristle 6; katepisternal setae 3; meroplueral setae 9; postalar wall setose; apical setae 2; subapical setae 2; distal scutellar setae 2; coxoplueral streak absent.
- *Wing* (Fig. 4.72): 5.97mm long and 3.04mm wide; I bare; tegula pale white; basicosta pale with black setae; r_{4+5} vein setose; costal spine absent; no subcoastal break; upper and lower calypter whitish and bare expect pale minute hairs at the margin.
- *Halter*: Dark brown with light brown knob.
- *Leg*: Black foreleg: 4.5mm long; coxa 0.65mm long, trochanter 0.36mm long, femur 0.91mm long, tibia 1.41mm long, tarsus 1.17mm long; mid leg: 7.88mm long; coxa 0.56mm long, trochanter 0.59mm long, femur 2.25mm long, tibia 2.13mm long, tarsus 2.35mm long.
- *Hind leg* (Fig. 4.74): 7.46mm long; coxa 1.37mm long, trochanter 0.44mm long, femur 2.31mm long, tibia 1.73mm long double fringed, tarsus 1.61mm long.

- *Abdomen* (Fig. 4.73): 4.50mm long and 2.39mm wide; abdomen with blackand grey patches along median stripe which is dark brown at 3rd tergite and light brown at 4th tergite; 4th tergite has marginal setae at the posterior margins of the segment; posterior margins of the 5th tergite thickly setose; genital segments I, II black.
- *Genitalia*: Terminalia round, black, densely covered with short setae at the end; 1-3 sternites are quadrangular.
- *Host plant:* unknown.
- *Paratype:* 6 male, 5 female, coll. Divya Jadav. March-Sept., wing and legs on slide, Pinned insects, labeled as above.
- *Distribution:* 4 male, Ajara, 09-xi-2014; 2 male, Gaganbawda, 28 -vii-2014; 1 female, Kolhapur, 10-iii-2014; 3 female, Shirol, 20-iv-2014; 1female, Ajara, 11-xi-2014.

ORDER - COLEOPTERA

FAMILY STAPHYLINIDAE

Subfamily Staphylininae

Creophilus Sp.

(Plate - XIII: Figs. 4.75-4.79)

- *Male* (Fig. 4.75-4.76): Body length 12.51mm long, 4.49mm wide; black to brownish; antenna 3.93 mm long; pronotum 2.88mm long and 3.29mm wide; elytra 3.86mm long and 2.46mm wide; abdomen 5.40mm in long and 3.72mm in wide; foreleg 6.44mm long, black.
- *Head* (Fig. 4.77): 2.21mm long, 2.20mm broad, frons 1.90mm wide; prognathous; shiny black characterized by the presence of yellow-gray setae on the posterior angles; eyes brownish red; eye 1.45mm long, 1.21mm wide; presence of erect long black setae marginally.
- *Antenna* (Fig. 4.78): 1.45mm long; thick, beaded, filiform with club; composed of 11 segments; blackish except at the tips which is pale brown; each segment consist of short brown hairs.
- *Thorax*: Pronotum 1.14 mm long and 1.40mm wide, margin is marked by pale yellow setae; than longer than broarder; prosternum 1.69mm long and 2.27mm wide; scutellum small, triangular, 1.01mm long, 1.00mm broad; mesosternum 0.88mm long and 2.55mm wide; metasternum 2.54mm long, 2.80mm wide.
- *Wing*: Elytra 3.86mm long and 2.46mm wide; cover the first few abdominal segments; golden brownish hairy.
- *Legs:* Legs moderately long, femora swollen; tarsai 4; foreleg 6.44mm long, coxa 1.63mm long, trochanter 0.09mm long, femur 1.96mm long, tibia 1.98mm long, tarsi 0.78mm long; mid leg: 9.13mm long, coxa 1.09mm

Plate – XII *S. orientalis* (69-74): Fig. 4.69: **Adult-dorsal view,** Fig. 4.70: **Adult-lateral view,** Fig. 4.71: **Head,** Fig. 4.72: **Wing,** Fig. 4.73: **Abdomen,** Fig. 4.74: **Hind leg**

long, trochanter 0.81mm long, femur 02,23mm long, tibia 2.51mm long, tarsi 2.49mm long.

- *Hind leg* (Fig. 4.79): 8.47mm long, coxa 1.12mm long, trochanter 1.12mm long, femur 1.81mm long, tibia 1.98mm long, tarsi 2.44mm long.
- *Abdomen*: 1.90mm in length and 1.77mm in width with visible 6 abdominal segments; posterior margin of the each segment is setose.
- *Host plant:* unknown.
- *Paratype:* 2 male, 3 female, coll. Divya Jadav. Mar.-May, wing and legs on slide, Pinned insects, labeled as above.
- *Distribution:* 2 male, Radhanagari, 08-III-2014; 1 female, Karveer, 10-II-2014. 3 female, Karveer, 10-IV- 2014.

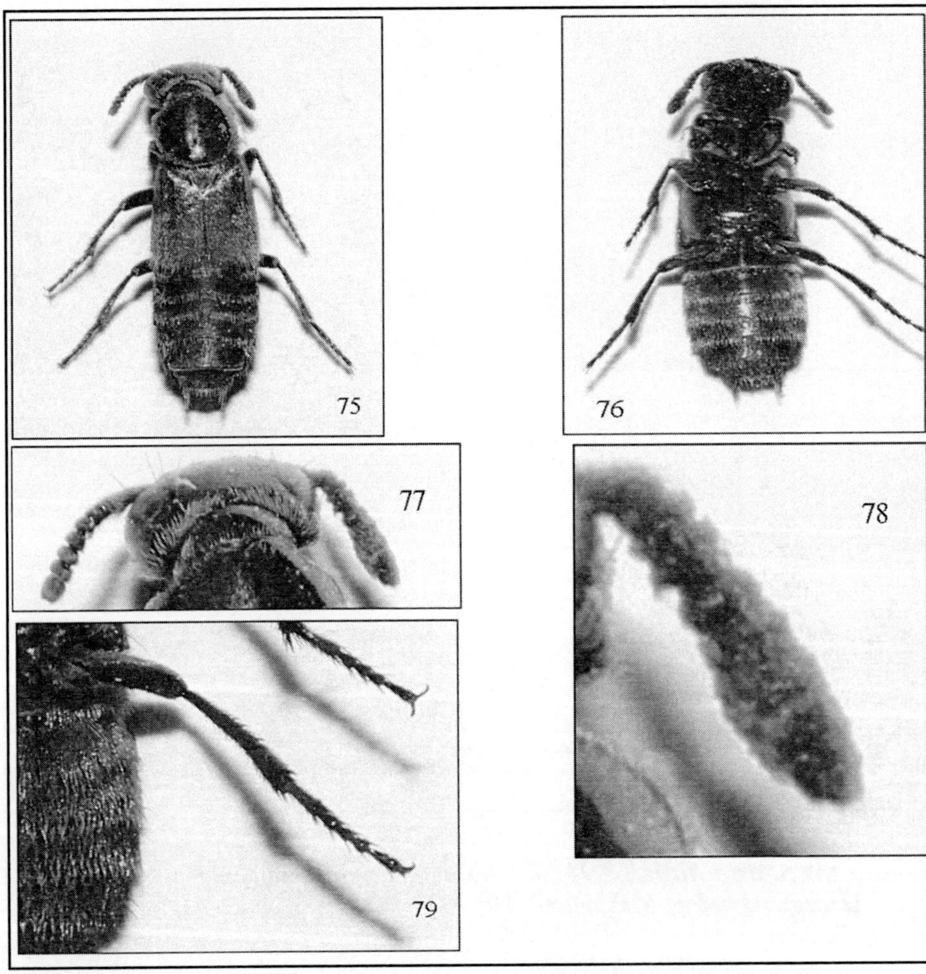

Plate – XIII *Creophilus sp.* (75-79): Fig. 4.75: **Adult-dorsal view,** Fig. 4.76: **Adult-ventral view,** Fig. 4.77: **Head,** Fig. 4.78: **Antenna,** Fig. 4.79: **Hind leg**

FAMILY CLERIDAE
SUBFAMILY CLEROIDEA
Necrobia rufipes (De Geer, 1775)

(Plate - XIV: Figs. 4.80-4.84)

- *Male* (Fig. 4.80): Body length 5.22mm long, width 2.44mm long; metallic green; antenna 1.45mm long; pronotum 1.14 mm long and 1.40mm wide; elytra 3.25mm long and 1.49mm wide; 1.90mm in long and 1.77mm in wide; foreleg 3.25mm long, black.
- *Head* (Fig. 4.81): 0.71mm long, 1.06mm broad, frons width- 0.64mm; head metallic green with sparsely punctured marked on frons and frontal striata with irregularly spreaded black, erect pubescence; median portion of frons and vertex with very few punctures; eyes reddish brown; eye length-0.41mm and eye width-0.32mm.
- *Antenna* (Fig. 4.82): 1.45mm long; base of the antenna is light orange which proceeds darker towards tip; clavate antennae with eleven segments; first thick, slightly bent and 0.20mm long; second 0.03mm long; third segment is 0.06 mm almost twice the length of second; fourth to eighth mutually equal in length, each just wider than the one preceding towards tip; ninth, tenth and eleventh segments transverse, subequal and strong; the eleventh almost square.
- *Thorax*: Pronotum 1.14 mm long and 1.40mm wide; broarder than longer; prosternum 1.02 mm long and 1.50mm wide; surface is with moderately coarse punctures; punctures much more dense at sides than on disc; pubescence as on head; scutellum small, transverse; mesosternum 0.81mm long and 1.45mm wide; metasternum 0.65mm long and 1.48mm wide.
- *Wing:* Elytra 3.25mm long and 1.49mm wide, surface is finely punctured and covered with pale golden short erect setae; margins with black pubescence.
- *Legs:* Legs moderately long, femora not enlarged tibiae straight, tarsi short with five segments of which the fourth is very small and concealed between the lobes of the third, first three segments with lamelliform pads beneath. claws rather long, provided at base with a broad tooth like appendage; foreleg 3.25mm long, coxa 0.23mm long, trochanter 0.18mm long, femur 0.95mm long, tibia 1.16mm long, tarsi 0.73mm long; mid leg: 3.18mm long, coxa 0.49mm long, trochanter 0.14mm long, femur 0.93mm long, tibia 1.01mm long, tarsi 0.63mm long.
- *Hind leg* (Fig. 4.83): 4.05mm long, coxa 0.24mm long, trochanter 0.52mm long, femur 1.06mm long, tibia 1.23mm long, tarsi 0.82mm long.
- *Abdomen* (Fig. 4.84): 1.90 mm in length and 1.77mm in width with visible 4 abdominal segments.

- *Host plant:* Brinjal.
- *Paratype:* 1 male, 6 female, coll. Divya Jadav. Feb.-May. wing and legs on slide, Pinned insects, labeled as above.
- *Distribution:* 7 male, Shirol, 22-V-2014; 7 male, Shirol, 22-V-2014.

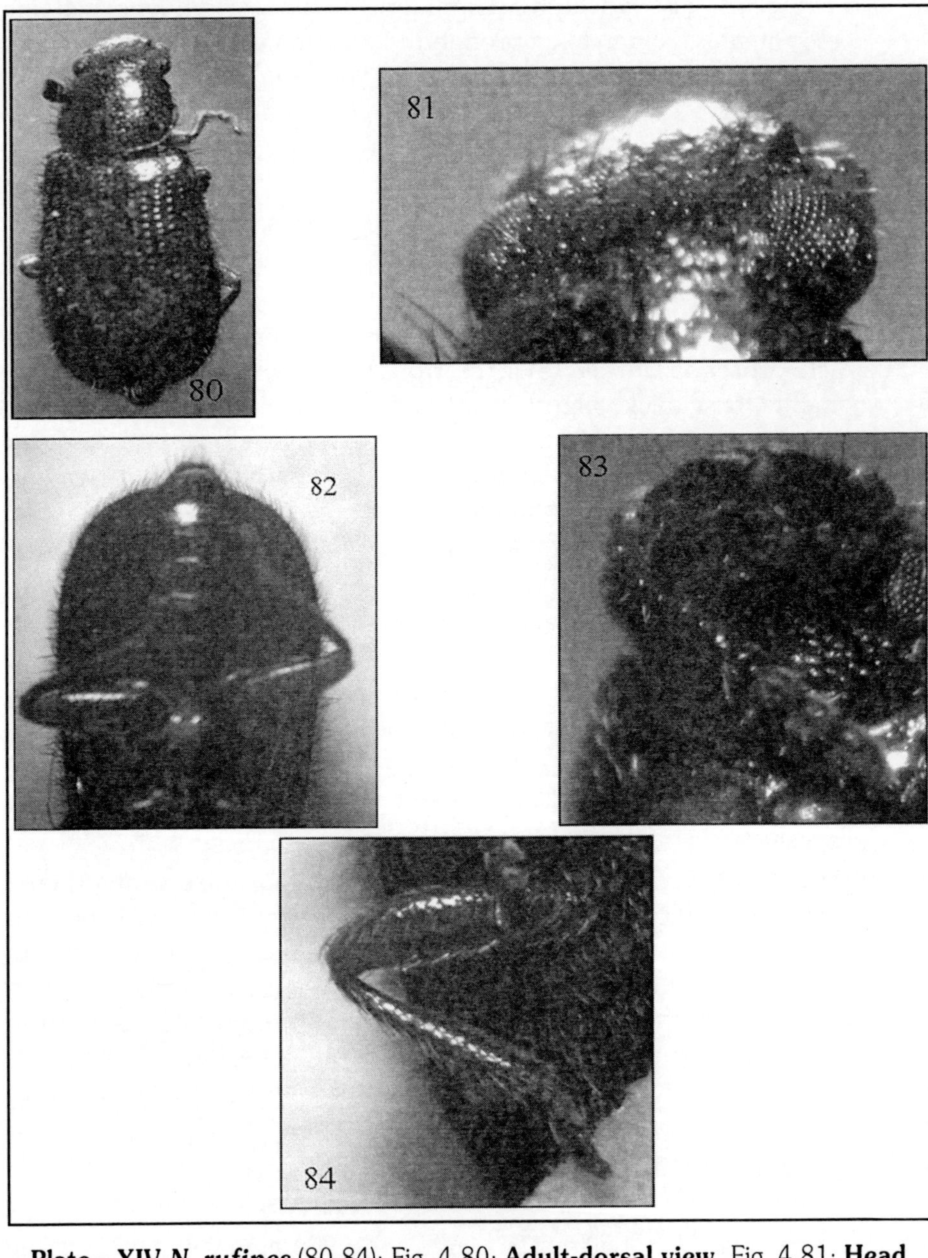

Plate – XIV *N. rufipes* (80-84): Fig. 4.80: **Adult-dorsal view,** Fig. 4.81: **Head,** Fig. 4.82: **Abdomen ventral view,** Fig. 4.83: **Hind leg**

FAMILY SILPHIDAE

SUBFAMILY SILPHINAE

Necrophila rufithorax (Wiedemann, 1823)

(Plate - XV: Figs. 4.85-4.89)

- *Male* (Fig. 4.85): Body length 21.43mm long, 8.92mm wide; antenna 4.04mm long; pronotum orange, 5.73mm long, 8.92mm wide; elytra 13.65mm long and 5.45mm wide; abdomen 9.40mm in long and 8.86mm in wide; foreleg 3.25mm long, black.
- *Head* (Fig. 4.86): 2.05mm long, 2.36mm broad; frons width 1.82mm; head blackish with sparsely spreader orange hairs near the mouth parts and at the edges of frons; median portion of frons and vertex with very few black spots on grey background; eyes reddish brown, eye 0.56 mm long and 0.55mm wide.
- *Antenna* (Fig. 4.87): 4.04mm long; dark brown; clavate with eleven segments; the first thick, slightly bent and 0.78mm long; the second 0.55mm long; third segment is 0.30 mm long and is quite elongate than other segments which is from fourth to sixth mutually equal in length; from seventh each just wider than the one preceding towards tip; ninth, tenth and eleventh segments transverse, subequal and strong; eleventh almost triangular.
- *Thorax:* Pronotum 5.73 mm length and 8.92mm width, broader than longer; orange with 4 black spots; it has a dark brown patch, out of 4 spots two are in brown patch and other two on orange portions of pronotum; prosternum 1.61mm length and mm 4.29 width; scutellum small and triangular with length 2.13mm and 3.66mm width; 3.08mm long and 6.56mm width of mesosternum; 1.64mm long and 6.26mm wide of metasternum; punctured around the pronotum except at the mid disc on brown patch.
- *Wings:* Elytra 13.65mm long and 5.45mm wide; elytra with 3 transverse line with punctured spots; presence of green reflections on elytra, elytra blunt at its end, ventrally elytra shoes peacock; hind wing 17.28mm long and 4.82mm broad, brownish in colour.
- *Legs:* Moderately long, black, femora not enlarged, tibiae straight, tarsi short, of five segments. claws rather long, provided at base with a broad tooth like appendage: fore leg (Fig. 4.89): 10.1mm long, coxa 1.72mm long, trochanter 1.07 mm long, femur 3.41mm long, tibia 1.62mm long, tarsi 2.28mm long. mid leg: 11.50mm long, coxa 0.75mm long, trochanter 0.70mm long, femur 3.34mm long, tibia 4.05mm long, tarsi 2.66mm long; hind leg: 15.54mm long, coxa 1.89mm long, trochanter 1.47mm long, femur 4.10mm long, tibia 4.99mm long, tarsi 3.09mm long.

- *Abdomen* (Fig. 4.88): 9.40mm in length and 8.86mm in width with visible 4-5 abdominal segments. From Third segments have golden marginal hair at the posterior side of the abdomen ventrally.
- *Host plant:* Brinjal.
- *Paratype:* 1 male, 1 female, coll. Divya Jadav. Feb.-May. Wing and legs on slide, Pinned insects, labeled as above.
- *Distribution:* 1 male, Radhanagari, 08-III-2014; 1 female, Karveer, 10-II-2014.

Plate – XV (85-89): Fig. 4.85: **Adult-dorsal view,** Fig. 4.86: **Head dorsal view,** Fig. 4.87: **Abdomen ventral view,** Fig. 4.88: **Antenna,** Fig. 4.89: **Fore leg**

ORDER COLEOPTERA

FAMILY HISTERIDAE

SUBFAMILY HISTERINAE

Saprinus splendens (Paykull, 1811)

(Plate - XVI: Figs. 4.90-4.94)

- *Male* (Fig. 4.90): Body 9.34mm long and 4.17mm broad, oval and convex; cuticle with metallic green shining; pronotum black; elytra light blue or green metallic luster; funicle of the antennae and tarsi dark brown; tibia black.
- *Head* (Fig. 4.91): 0.96 mm long, 1.43mm broad; frons 0.97mm wide, head black with fine small puncture; frons rectangular in shape; the median portion of frons and vertex with very few black punctures; eyes black; eye 0.64 mm in length and 0.38mm in width.
- *Antenna* (Fig. 4.92): 0.87mm long; the antenna is dark brown, clubbed antennae with first segment 0.24mm long, second 0.05mm 3-6 segments very small 0.28mm in length, last segment clubbed, oval and thick with 0.30mm long and 0.34mm width.
- *Thorax*: Pronotum 2.06mm long and 4.17mm broad; broader than longer; shiny bluish black; scutellum small and triangular with 0.14 mm long and 0.03mm wide; prosternum 1.49mm long and 0.69mm wide; 2.36mm long and 3.09mm wide of mesosternum; 1.51mm long and 2.62mm wide of metasternum; punctured around the pronotum except at the mid disc.
- *Wings*: Elytra 3.49mm long and 2.73mm wide; widest at their end; three external dorsal stria reaching the middle of elyptra while fourth stria shorter; elyptral punctuation is dense, irregular size and present throughout the elytra except at the medial disc which is shiny; presence of green reflections on elytra.
- *Legs:* Moderately long, black; femora and tibia enlarged and strong; tarsi short of five segments; profemur with large punctures which are larger than meso - and meta femoral punctures; protibia with three small apical teeth followed by seven marginal ones; all femora with row of setae on their outer margin; foreleg (Fig. 4.94) coxa 0.62mm long, trochanter 0.42mm long, femur 1.57mm long, tibia 1.56mm long, tarsi 0.97mm long; mid leg: coxa 0.62mm long, trochanter 0.56mm long, femur 1.71mm long, tibia 1.70mm long, tarsi 1.15mm long; hind leg: coxa 0.69mm long, trochanter 0.50mm long, femur 1.24mm long, tibia 1.48mm long, tarsi 1.04mm long.
- *Abdomen* (Fig. 4.93): 2.56mm long and 3.69mm wide with visible 4-5 abdominal segments. each segments have punctuation at the posterior margin of the abdomen ventrally.

- *Host plant:* unknown.
- *Paratype:* 3 female, coll. Divya Jadav. Jan - May, wing and legs on slide, Pinned insects, labeled as above.
- *Distribution:* 3 Female, Radhanagari, 18-I-2014;1 female , Kolhapur, 3-V- 2014.

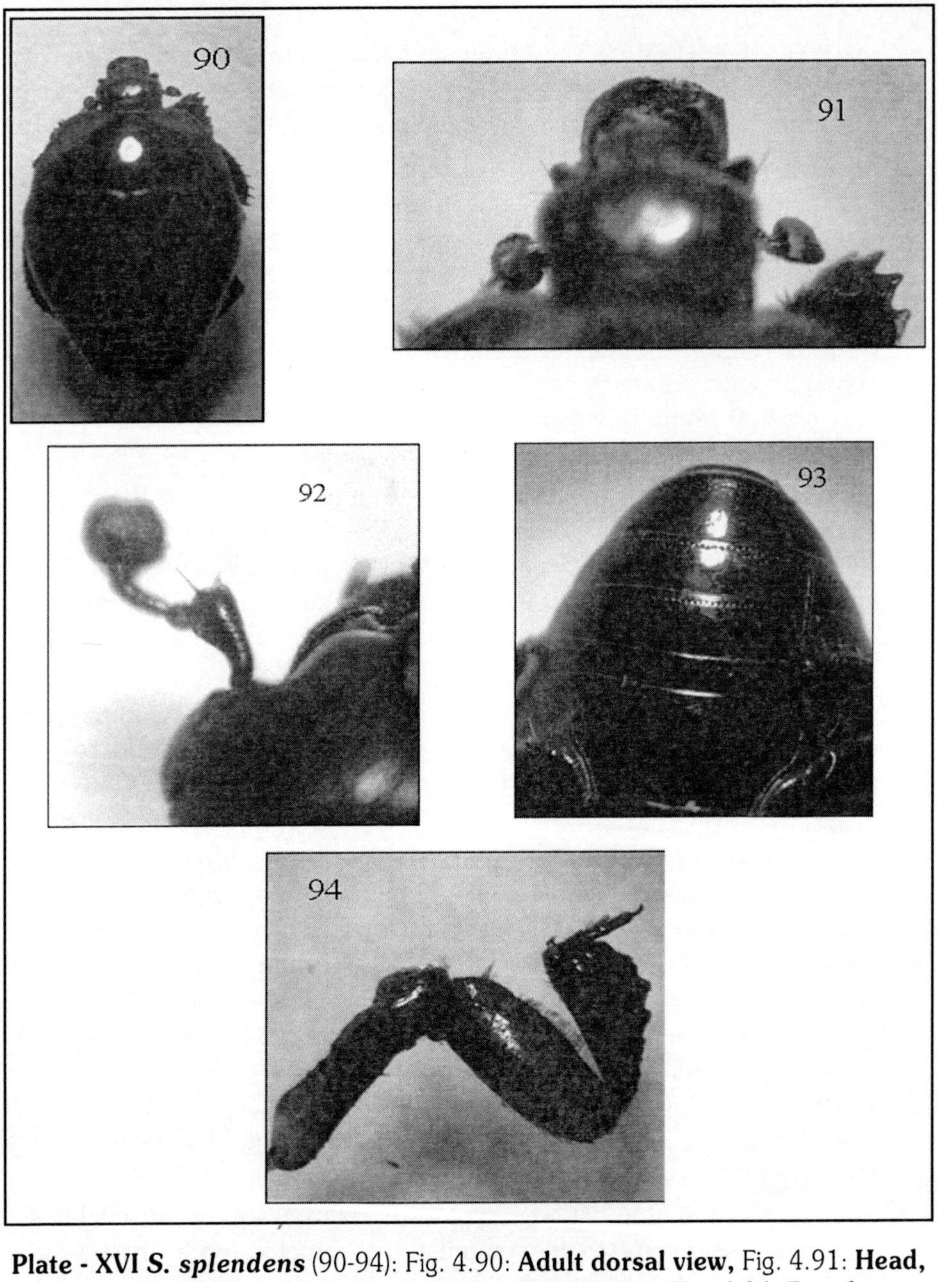

Plate - XVI *S. splendens* (90-94): Fig. 4.90: **Adult dorsal view,** Fig. 4.91: **Head,** Fig. 4.92: **Antenna,** Fig. 4.93: **Abdomen ventral view,** Fig. 4.94: **Fore leg**

Wasp-Hymenoptera

(Plate - XVII: Figs. 4.95-4.99) (See Page no. 72)

- *Male* (Fig. 4.95): Body long 11.77mm, 4.15mm wide; wing 3.56mm long and 1.27mm wide; antenna 1.15mm long, 0.35mm broad; thorax 2.29mm long, 0.93mm broad; 4.03mm long and 1.01mm wide.
- *Head* (Fig. 4.96): 2.71mm long, 1.10 mm broad, blackish orange; black eyes; eye facets are small and uniform, 1.86mm long, 1.35mm broad; presence of outer and inner vertical setae; frontal wide 0.65mm; no forntal vittae dark brown to blackish towards vertex with a row of 5-6 setalue along its external margin reaching the level of ocellar triangle; genal dilation creamy with few black setae near the facial ridge; vibrissa and subvibrissal setule black; palpi orange.
- *Antenna*: Reddish brown; 1.15mm long, 0.35mm broad; scape black 0.09mm long, 0.15mm wide, pedicle dark brown- 0.24mm long, 0.21mm wide, first flagellomere dark brown 0.82mm long, 0.35mm wide; arista plumose.
- *Flagellar formula*: S L/W: 0.6, P L/W: 1.14, F L/W: 2.34, Average: 1.36.
- *Thorax* (Fig. 4.97): 2.29mm in long, 0.93mm broad; proscutem- 0.74mm long, 0.93mm in wide; scutem- 0.92mm long, 0.93mm in wide; scutellum- 0.49mm long, 0.48mmin wide.
- *Wing* (Fig. 4.98): 3.56mm in long and 1.27 mm in wide. hyaline; tegula and basicosta brown.
- *Legs* (Fig. 4.99): Thin, long, creamy brownish.
- *Abdomen:* Abdomen 4.03mm long and 1.01mm wide; with blackish spots on creamy brown abdomen.
- *Host plant:* unknown.
- *Paratype:* 1 male, coll. Divya Jadav. Feb.-May. wing and legs on slide, Pinned insects, labeled as above.
- *Distribution:* 1 male, Radhanagari, 08-III-2014; 1 female , Karveer, 10-II-2014.

ORDER ANAPLEURA

FAMILY PEDICULIDAE

Head Louse - *Pediculus humanus* De Geer, 1767

(Plate - XVIII: Figs. 4.100-4.101)

- *Male* (Fig.121-122): 1.88mm long, 0.64mm broad; pale creamy brown in colour; wingless insect.
- *Head*: 0.48mm long, 0.32mm broad; longer than broader; pale creamy brown in colour; antennae with five segments, protrude from the head; eyes are black 0.04mm long and 0.02mm wide.

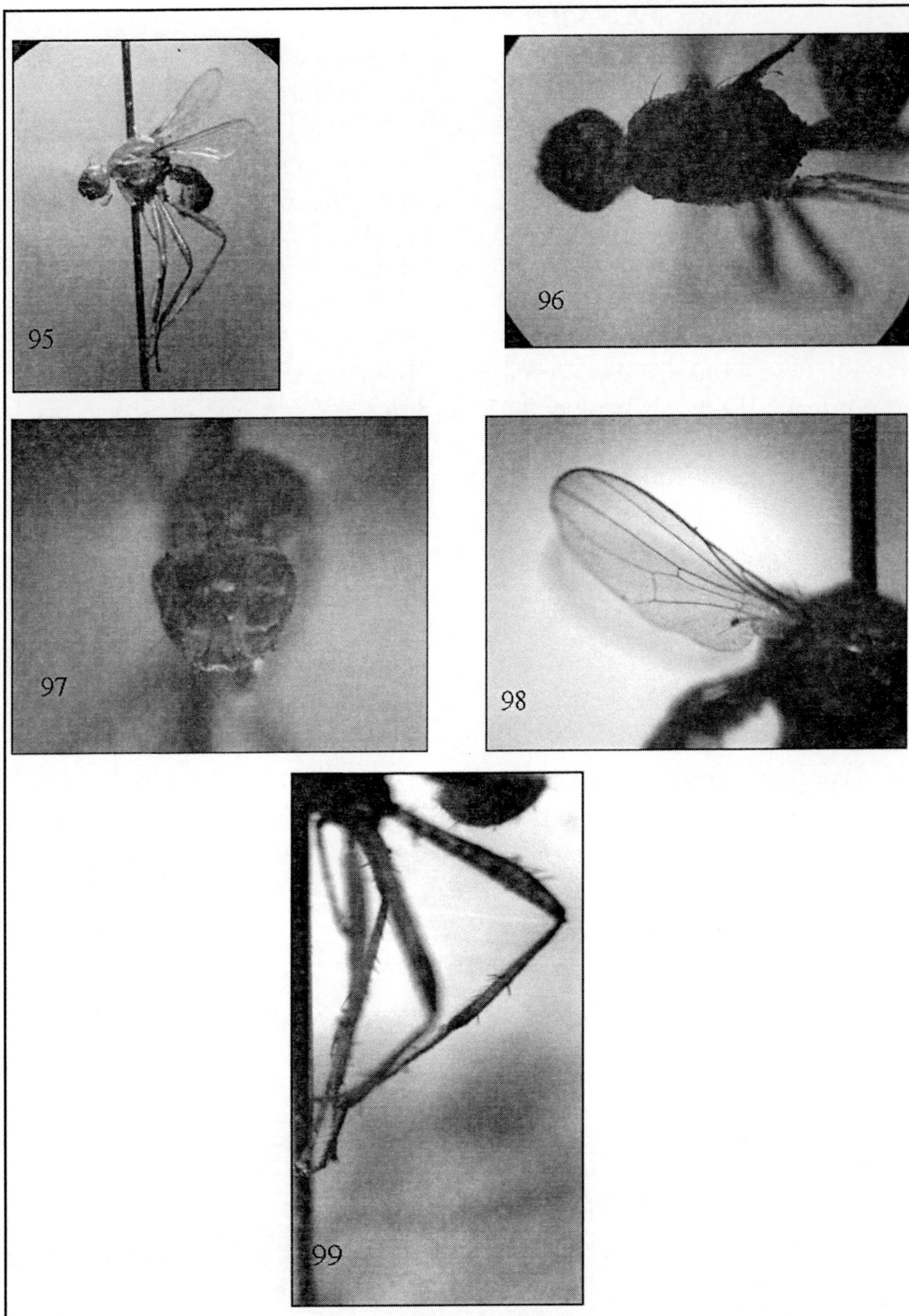

Plate – XVII Wasp (Hymenoptera) (95-99): Fig. 4.95: **Adult-dorsal view,** Fig. 4.96: **Thorax dorsal view,** Fig. 4.97: **Head,** Fig. 4.98: **Wing,** Fig. 4.99: **Legs**

- *Antenna:* Five segmented; 0.32mm long light brown in colour.
- *Thorax:* 0.32mm long, 0.44mm broad; legs are short and terminate with a single claw with a thumb.
- *Abdomen:* 1.08mm long, 0.64mm broad with seven visible segments; tergite margins are blackish.
- *Genitalia*: In male lice, the front two legs are slightly larger than the other four. Males are small and are characterised by a pointed end of the abdomen and a well-developed genital apparatus visible inside the abdomen. Females are characterised by two gonopods in the shape of a W at the end of their abdomen.
- *Host plant:* unknown.
- *Paratype:* 1 male, 2 female, coll. Divya Jadav. May.-June. wing and legs on slide, Pinned insects, labeled as above.
- *Distribution:* 1 male, Radhanagari, 08-V-2014; 2 female, Karveer, 10-VI-2014.

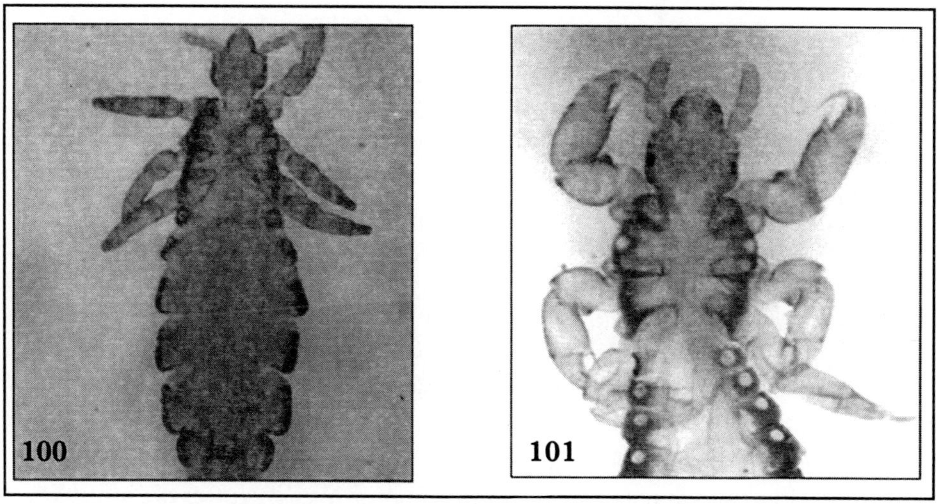

Plate - XVIII: *P. humanus* (100-101): Fig. 4.100: **Adult-dorsal view,** Fig. 4.101: **Adult-lateral view**

5 BIOLOGY OF FORENSIC INSECTS

INTRODUCTION

Biology of an organism plays a very crucial role in experimental work especially in forensic science. Forensic or medico-criminal entomology is a major field of forensic sciences. Forensic entomology is inexorably a scientific discipline that interprets the information related to death using insect specimens as silent witness in order to provide data not available by using the routine methods of classic pathology (Wolff *et al.* 2001). The first record of use of insects in crime investigation dates back to 13th century from a Chinese village (Mc knight, 1981). During the last three decades, the utility of medico-criminal entomology in death investigations has been largely documented by several case studies in western countries mainly the Europe and U.S.A (Nuorteva, *et al.* 1967), were among the first to use forensic entomology for determination of PMI. In Europe and many countries of the world forensic entomology was widely accepted by the beginning of 21st century.

A wide variety of insects have forensic value since they visit and colonize a body at different stages of decomposition and may include: flies (Diptera), beetles (Coleoptera), bees, wasps, ants (Hymenoptera), butterflies and moths (Lepidoptera), lice, cockroaches and several others. The most important forensic insect groups are: flesh flies, blowflies and beetles. About 2600 species of flesh flies (Sarcophagids) are reported from the world. They found associated with carcasses and involved in myiasis in man and animals (Byrd and Castner, 2010). Calliphoridae family provides 1100 described species of blow flies from the world (https://en.wikipedia.org/wiki/Calliphoridae). All beetle stages are important since they move fast and are often found under the body, or in and under clothing.

Review of literature indicates that Parker (1916), Papp (1971), Beaver (1972), Pickens (1981), Jiron and Bolanos (1986), Liu and Green burg (1989), Queiroz *et al.* (1997), Byrd and Castner (2001), Greenberg and Kunich (2002), Grassberger and Reiter (2002), Mendez and Papae (2002), Byrd-David *et al.* (2003), Lefebver and Pasquerault (2004), Gabre *et al.* (2005), Singh and Sharma (2008), Jadav and Sathe (2014), Majumder *et al.* (2014), etc., studied the biology of forensic insects.

MATERIALS AND METHODS

Two dipterous flies *Sacrophaga sera* Meigen and *Sarcophaga josephi* Bottcher (Sarcophagidae) and one coleopterous beetle *Saprinus splendens* (Peyk.) and have been selected for their biological studies. Biology (life cycle) of above insects have been studied under laboratory conditions (27±1°C, 75-80% RH, 12 hr photoperiod).

Life Cycle of Flies

Adult stock of flies was kept in rectangular cage (25 × 25 × 25cm) which was provided with nylon slew door. The flies were supplied with solution I of sugar and water soaked in cotton as food. Fresh goat liver was supplied to the adult flies for proper reproductive development. Initially, small pieces of fresh goat liver were given which helped the growth of reproductive system. The mated female were provided with goat flesh in small piece 4 × 4 inch as food in petridish, which was kept in glass cage for the developmental studies of flies. Within 18-24 hours larviposition was noticed on the flesh. The larvae feed on liquefied tissues. There were three stages in the larva. When third instar larva stopped its feeding it wandered away from the food supplied. Therefore, at the end of third instar, the petridish was kept open in the glass trough containing fine particulated soil layer at the base for pupation of larvae. The larvae pupated in the soil and then adult emerged from these pupae. Many times, once the larvae pupated, they were separated in plastic containers for adult emergence. Sufficient numbers of immature stages (larval instars and pupae) were collected with noting the duration of each stage including instars. The immatures have been morphologically featured by consulting compound microscope.

Beetle Life Cycle

More or less same rearing technique was used for studying life cycle of beetle species. The food and rearing equipments were same as noted above. However, adult beetles were kept in container in small groups for their maintenance. The beetle showed four distinct stages of its life cycle *viz;* egg, larva, pupa and adult. The beetle generally burry themselves in ground therefore, in plastic container a thin layer of soil have been arranged for keeping beetles in them.

Adult longevity of flies and beetles has been counted as per the method given in Chapter - III. While sex ratio of individual forensic insects was counted by counting the number of both sexes.

RESULTS

1. Flesh fly - *Sarcophaga josephi* Buttcher

The fly shows four distinct stages of life cycle *viz;* egg, larva, pupa and adult.

- *Egg*: The eggs were whitish, slightly curved and slightly narrow at one end. 20 eggs measured 1.50 mm in length 0.40 mm in width. Eggs matured in egg purse of female in body and hatched into 1st instar larvae in the body of female itself and then larviposition of 1st instar taken place. The incubation period was 2 days.
- *Larvae*: These are three instars in the larval stage.
  - *Ist instar* (Fig. 5.1): The 1st instar showed a translucent body which was tapering towards posteriorly. The larva was marked by a band of minute spiny bristles. The larviposition of 1st instar was on fresh meat of goat. But in natural condition, it was on the host animal tissues, specially on open wounds, ulcers or in the nostrils, where the larvae feed and burrow into the tissues. This stage lasted for one day. 10 individuals measured 1.60 mm in body length and 0.43 mm in width.
  - *2nd Instar* (Fig. 5.2): This instar was also tapering towards anteriorly and broader towards posteriorly and showed and with transverse bands of minute spiny bristles, 10 individuals measured 4.20 mm in body length and 0.85 mm in width. This stage lasted for one day.
  - *3rd Instar* (Fig. 5.3): There was significant increased size of third instar larva. 10 individuals measured 12.00 mm in body length and 4.2 mm in width. Morphological features of third instar were more or less similar to the previousinstar except the size. The colour of larva was deep creamy to yellowish brown. This stage lasted for two days. The total larval period from 1st instar to pupa was 5-6 days.
- *Pupa* (Fig. 5.4): The pupa was coarctate adecticous type. Pupa was broadly parallel sided and rounded from posterior side and slightly pointed from anterior side 10 individual pupae measured 11.00 mm in body length and 4.1 mm in width. The pupal period recorded was 5 to 6 days. The pupa was characterised by transverse bands of spines, blackish mouth hook which was more sclerotized.
- *Adult* (Fig. 5.5): Males were smaller than females. Newly emerged flies were soft and grayish black with thorax grey striped longitudinally

with black; eyes were red and abdomen was with 4 visible segments and with cheequered 'shot' patterns of dark and light grey. Antenna arista bare at the end. The tarsi were large sized.

- *Adult Longevity:* Males survived for 25 days and females for 32 days with sex ratio (male: female) (30:37) (1:1:22) favouring females.

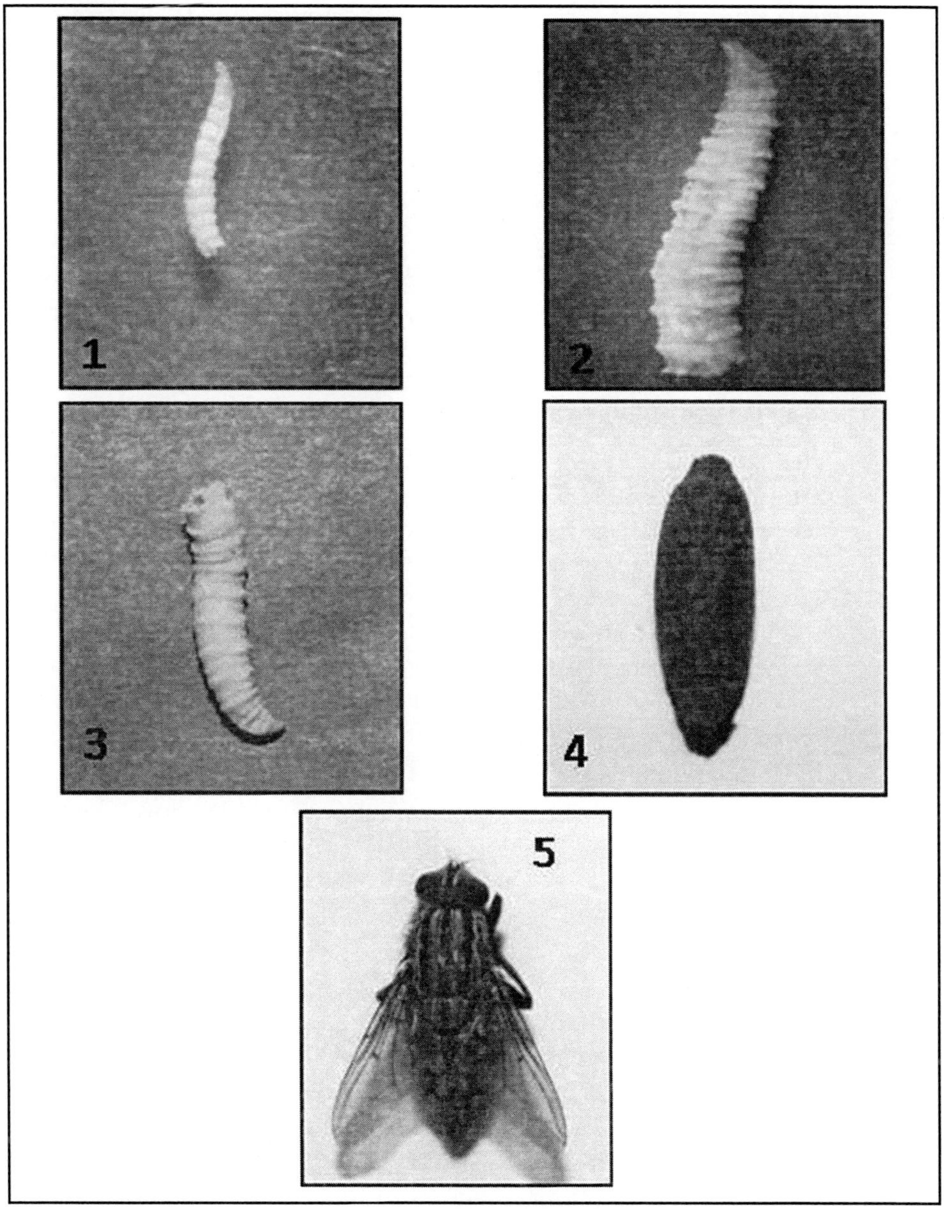

Plate - I: *Sarcophaga josephi:* Life cycle stages: Fig. 5.1: **First instar,** Fig. 5.2: **Second instar,** Fig. 5.3: **Third Instar,** Fig. 5.4: **Pupa,** Fig. 5.5: **Adult**

2. *Sarcophaga sera* Rodh.

- *Egg:* The uterian eggs were white, thin walled and typically rounded at both the ends. The uterian eggs hatched within 2-3 days in the body itself and larval forms were deposited in the tissues of host. The length and width of 10 eggs averaged 0.08mm (ranged 0.09 to 0.14mm) and 0.10mm (ranged 0.09-0.13mm) respectively. About 130 eggs were counted per female. Its cephalic end was broadened.
- *Instars:* The parasite showed 3 instars. All instars were apodous and non-vesiculated.
  - *Ist Instar* (Fig. 5.6): The first instar was with a translucent body and with small head and with dark mandibles. It shows 3 thoracic and 7 abdominal segments. After a day body became more opaque. The body length of 10 individuals averaged 1.20mm (range 1.00-1.30) and width was 0.30mm (range 0.28-0.35mm). In 10 individuals, mandibles averaged 0.30mm (range 0.027 to 0.033mm) and 0.010mm (range 0.008 to 0.012mm) in length and width respectively. First instar lasted for 1 to 2 days.
  - *IInd Instar* (Fig. 5.7): The body of second instar was cylindrical, straight and white. The integument of larva was very thin. The larva consisted a narrow head, 12 well defined segments and typical cauda tapering posteriorly. Tracheal system showed single lateral longitudinal trunk. A pair of prothoracic and posterior pair was seen in second instar larva. The average length and width of the body measured in 10 individuals were 2.10mm (range 2.00-2.30mm) and 0.70mm (range 0.68-0.72mm) respectively and the length of 10 mandibles averaged 0.051mm (range 0.047-0.053mm) and width 0.02mm (range 0.019-0.025mm). This stage lasted for 2-3 days.
  - *IIIrd Instar* (Fig. 5.8): This instar was more opaque yellow. The body segments were clearly seen. The larva consisted the head and 12 well defined segments and tapered towards anteriorly. In the late stage of 3rd instar the body became shortened, cauda was reduced. Third instar larva was with well-developed tracheal system. Tracheal system was with two longitudinal trunks and one transverse commissure. Thoracic and abdominal spiracles were in 3+5 pairs. The average body length and width of the body measured in 10 individuals were 2.5mm (range 2.40 to 2.55mm) and 0.60mm (range 0.58 to 0.65mm) respectively. The mandible length and width observed in 10 individuals averaged 0.075mm (range 0.073 to 0.080mm) and 0.031mm (range 0.029 to 0.033mm) respectively. The mouth parts were heavily sclerotized and well developed strong mandibles were found. This stage stayed for 3-4 days.

- *Pupa* (Fig. 5.9): Fully grown third instar of fly leave the host material and searched for a suitable space for pupation in soil. The third instar larva reduced in size and become whitish reaches prepupa (Fig. 5.9) stage The pupa was coarctate and adecticous type. At initial stage the body showed three distinct divisions. Later, appendages developed and its original white colour became darker and darker progressing its development. The pupa was in cocoon which was dark brownish, parallel sided and rounded at both ends but anterior end was slightly pointed. The pupal stage lasted for 5-7days.
- *Adult* (Fig. 5.10): Adult was blackish with 3 longitudinal greyish stripes on thorax. Female measured 12.36 mm in body length and 2.96 mm in width with a wing expanse of 9.72 mm. Males were smaller than females. Life cycle of this species from egg to adult was completed within 13 to 18 days. The adults survived for 3 days without food, males for 1.5 day and females for 2 days.

Life Cycle of Beetle *Saprinus splendens* (Payk.)

Beetles move fast on and around the carcasses. They always approach carcasses latter than the flesh flies and blowflies. This Histerid beetle has four distinct stages of life cycle *viz;* egg, larva (grub), pupa and adult. All beetle stages have forensic importance. The present species *S. splendens* was found associated with pig carcass in India. Therefore, the life studies of this beetle have tremendous importance in correlating life cycle with human hosts if any.

- *Egg:* Eggs are whitish, smooth, shining, translucent and rounded at both the ends. The average length and width measured in 10 individuals were 1.5mm and 0.40mm respectively. Incubation period was 2-3 days.
  - *Ist Instar*: The first instar was opaque yellow in colour, hairy and with 13 well defined segments. In 10 individuals early first instar larvae measured 1.7mm in length and 0.50mm in width and first instar larvae measured 2.5mm and 0.65mm in length and width respectively. This stage lasted for 3 days.
  - *IInd Instar:* This instar lasted for 4-8 days. These grubs were voracious feeders of animal tissues which go deep towards the bones. It was characterised by body darker colour, more hairy and larger size. In 10 individuals of early stage, larvae measured 3.2 mm in body length and 1.4 mm in width.

The larvae were found somewhat specialized in feeding habit that then made tunnels in tissue and holes on the host material. The grubs were voracious feeders. In 10 individuals late instar measured 4.5mm in body length and 3.20mm in width. The opaque body was darker in this stage and the grub was with prominent hairs and with 3 thoracic and 5 abdominal spiracle pairs.

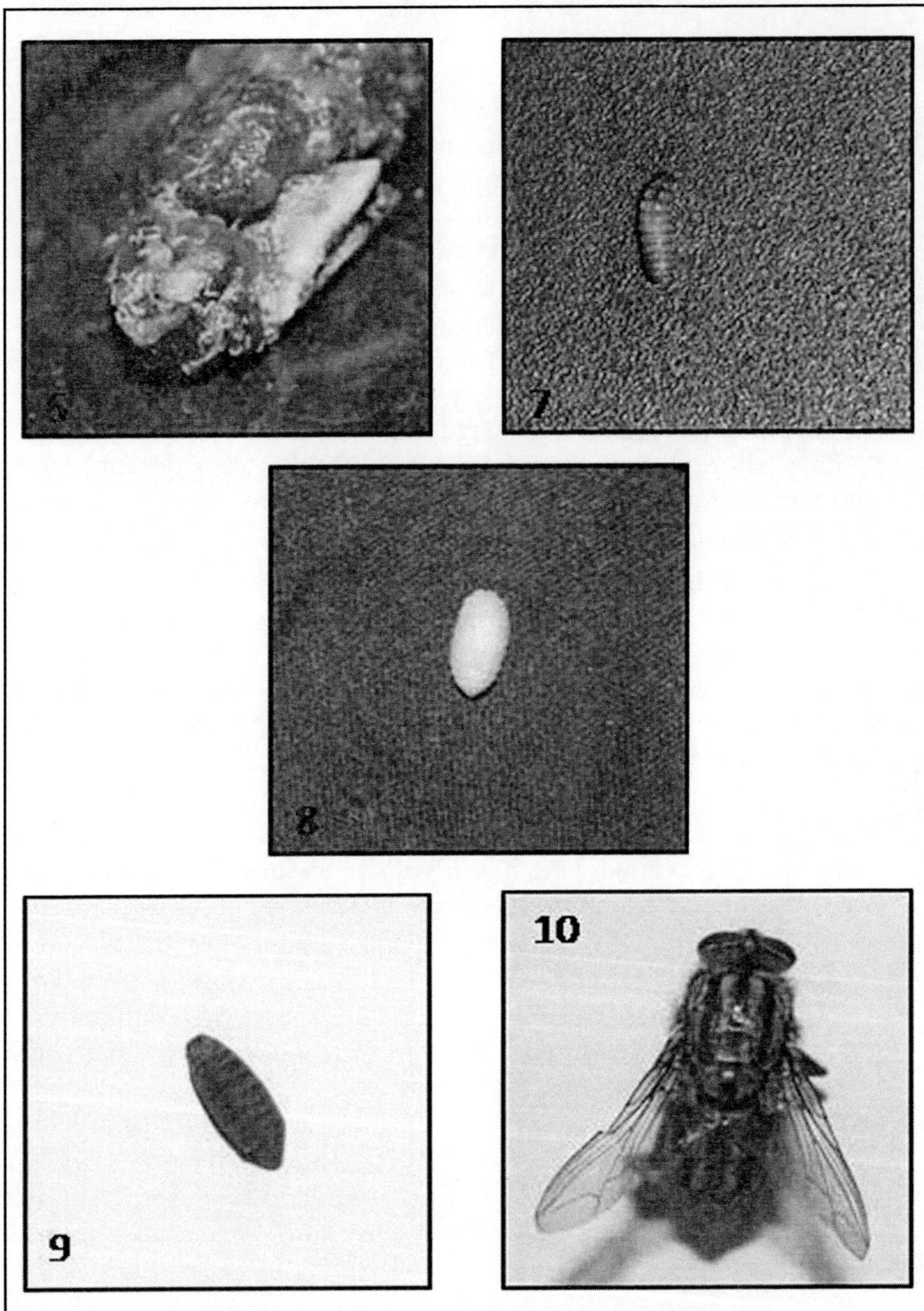

Plate - II: ***Sarcophaga sera:*** **Life cycle stages:** Fig. 5.6: **First instar,** Fig. 5.7: **Second instar,** Fig. 5.8: **Prepupa,** Fig. 5.9: **Pupa,** Fig. 5.10: **Adult**

Tracheal system was prominent with longitudinal trunks. Mandibles were dark and strong. The body of the grub was darkened to brownish colour and with very prominent hairs. The grubs were found boring into the bones and were largely associated with bones and bone tissues. Fully grown grub left the semiaquatic medium and searched dry place for pupation.

- *Pupa*: The second instar larva reduced in its length and became broader for prepupation. The prepupa showed three distinct divisions of the body *viz*; head thorax and abdomen and was whitish in colour. No appendages were found in prepupa. Prepupal skin was casted and pupa was formed with initial light colour but later became darker and darker and finally brownish black with all well-developed appendages of head, thorax and abdomen. In 10 individuals of pupae measured 4.40mm in length and 3.30mm in width. The prepupal stage and pupal stage was lasted for 2-3days and 5-6 days respectively. The total life cycle was completed within 20-25 days.
- *Adult*: Males were smaller than females. Adults were characterized by having black shining body colour, measuring about 4.5-5.5mm and width 3.5-4.5 mm. Pronotum with large shiny disc. Protibia with 6 blunt dentrites but not pointed.

Discussion

The biological diversity of Diptera is remarkable (Courtney *et al.* 2009). Despite its great importance, the immature larval instars of many families of this order are little known and even more complicated on those group of which taxonomy is unstable in adult stage (Mendez and Pape, 2002; Szpila and Pape, 2008). Since sarophagids are considered as potential indicators of the time of death, interest in larval developmental studies have been increased (Perez-Moreno *et al.* 2006; Buenaentura *et al.* 2009). The development time of the species is the reference point for dating the death (Ames and Turner, 2003). Therefore, biological information of the species involved in the case has prime importance in forensic science.

Peckia (P.) *chrysostoma* has been found during the advance stage of decomposition of carcasses in the Cerrado area of Brazilian Federal District (Barros, *et.al.* 2008) as well as in flesh stage in Colombian Amazon (Pape *et al.* 2004). It has also been recognized as an important species from the view of forensic value from South America.

Sukontason *et al.* (2006) made morphological comparison between *Chrysomya rufifacies* (Mac.) and *C. villeneuri* Patton (Calliporidae) puparia. They reported that a larger number of globules at the bubble membrane on the dorsolateral border of fifth segment was found in *C. villeneuni* (ave.225) than in *C. rufifacies* (ave.35) and more papillae was observed on the anterior spiracle in *C. villeneuni* (13-15) than in *C. rufifacies* (9-12).

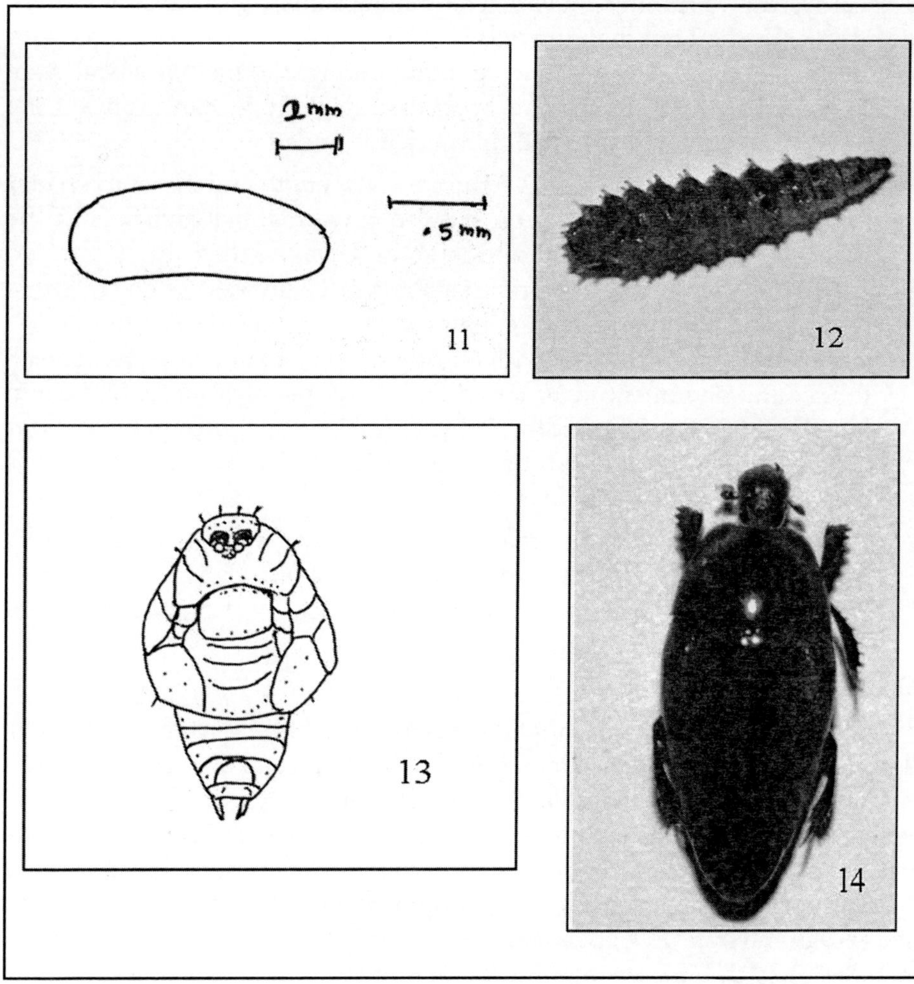

Plate – III: *S. splendens:* Life cycle stages (11-14): Fig. 5.11: **Egg,** Fig. 5.12: **Second instar larva,** Fig. 5.13: **Pupa,** Fig. 5.14: **Adult**

Kamal (1958) studied the bionomics of green bottle *Lucilia sericata* and European blue bottle *Calliphora vicina* easily rearable on beef liver at 27±1°C and 50±2 per cent RH with continuous light (ordinarily incandescent bulbs). He reported 18 days and 12 days as an average period for immature stages of the flies. He also noted the adult life span as 25 days and 46 days in *C. vicina* and *L. sericata* respectively.

The blow fly eggs are usually very shiny and white, ranging in size from around 0.9 mm to over 1.50 mm long and 0.3-0.4 mm wide (Rognes, 1991). According to Erzinclioglu (1996) in *C. vicina* fertilization was occurred without availability of oviposition site and live larviposition was common thing. Larviposition on food material was also found in present forms (flies). Similarly, the larva showed 12 segments in its body and was pointed anteriorly and broader posteriorly with black coloured mandibles. There were 3 instars in above species. Similarly, in present flies 3 instars were reported in larval stage.

Beetles have complete metamorphosis with four distinct stages of life cycle *viz;* egg, grub (larva), pupa and adult. The beetles show oval, spherical or spheroid shaped eggs. The length of the life cycle in forensic beetle is vary with the species. In rove beetle (Staphylindae) development from egg to adult was completed within 7-10 days, while, in ground beetles (Carbidae) it has been extended to one year and the adults may live for 2-3 years (Hinton, 1945). However, there is only one generation in a single year in many forensic beetles. The pupal period in *Dermester* sp. was 2 weeks to months.

Watson and Carlton (2005) investigated the life cycle of three American beetles *viz; Oiceoptomaina equale* (Fab.), *Necrophilia Americana* (Lin.) and *Necrodes surinamensis* (Fab.). They identified 3 larval stages. The first, second and third instars averaged for 12 days, 10 days and 11 days respectively in *N. surnamensis*. In the present study, the histerid beetle showed three instars and its life cycle was completed within 20-25 days at 27±1°C, 75-80 per cent RH and 12 hr photoperiod.

According to Majumder *et al.* (2013) the variation in dietary proteins and paired and unpaired condition influenced the adult longevity in *B. peregrine*. The longevity of male was always greater than female in the both paired and unpaired condition irrespective of variation in dilatory proteins and paired and unpaired condition influenced the adult longevity in *B. peregrine.* The longevity of both males was always greater than females in the both paired and unpaired conditions irrespective of variation in food sources. In *C. megacephala*, the adult longevity of both males and females feeding on liver was always more prolonged than those reared on the food without liver. Protein rich food, such as: fresh bovine liver was essential for the reproductive development of *B. perqrina* (Gabare *et al.* 2005) while, Majumder *et al.* (2012) noted that 'fresh fish' as a food for *B. perearina* was also found useful.

According to Shiravi *et al.* (2011) in general, in flesh fly Sarcophaga sp. the development rates were lower than blow flies *L. sericata* and *C. albiceps*. These rates for Sarcophaga sp. were 0.33-0.50, 0.16-0.20 and 0.10-0.16 for eggs, larvae and pupae respectively. The flesh fly required more heat for development than the blow flies mentioned above.

Preliminary observations on the biology of *Necrobia rufipes* were carried out by Simmons and Zllington (1925). They made some observations on biology and behaviour and gave general account of egg hatching, larvae, pupae and adults and also discussed fecundity and development. The fecundity was an average of 137 eggs and the incubation period was 4-5 days.

Osuji (1975) studied the development of *Dermestes maculates* in dried fish under uncontrolled laboratory conditions in Nigeria. He reported that the female laid eggs within 12 hours of copulation and oviposition was improved by the presence of free water. The larvae development was completed within 33.5 days within 7 months and the adults were emerged in about 11 days after the end of the last larval instar.

Osuji (1978) made comparative assessment of the biological performance of *D. maculates* in various dietary media namely: dried fish, fish meal, bone meal, palm kenel meal, blood meal and whole meal; the dried fish followed by fish meal and suggested the greater suitability of dried fish diet in development of the beetle.

According to Bhuiyan and Saifullah (1997) the average longevity of adults was found to be 60.64 ± 39.46 days for females and 49.42 ± 18.2 days for males with mean fecundity of female 89.7 ± 17.8 eggs when fed with a mixture of dried fish and copra as food.

Nath and Pande (1996) studied the biology of *D. maculatus* under uncontrolled laboratory conditions by providing dried fish in north-east India. They noted preovipositon, oviposition and post ovipositon periods as 5-6 days, 40-47 days and 8-10 days respectively and the fecundity varied from 29-95. They also noted that the adults were long lined and polygamous.

The speed of development in the flesh fly was slower than blow flies (Shiravi *et al.* 2011). This finding has important in forensic entomology and PMI where *Sarcophaga* sp presents. Total development time of *Sarcophaga* sp from first instar larvae to adult emergence reared at 28°C was 13-19 days which was similar to the development time, 16.4 days of *Sarcophaga dux* reared at the same temperature (28°C) (Al-Misned, 2003). Total development time of *C. albiceps* from egg to adult was 8-12 days when reared at 28°C which was similar to those (9.5-10.5 days) reported by Marchenko (2001). The variation of development times between different populations emphasises on specific characterization of regional development times of species (Shiravi, *et al.* 2011).

Green (1951) studied the behaviour of larvae of blowfly in the field and observed that they could travel distance of 6-10 m from the centre of dispersal.

Nutrition plays very crucial role in life activities which affect, development, longevity, physiology, reproduction, sex ratio, genetics and survival (Sathe and Margaj, 2001). Natural or synthetic diet, humidity and competition between larvae have tremendous importance in rearing of forensic insects. The effect of diet on development of flies has been studied by various workers (Kaneshrajah and Turner, 2004; Clark *et al.* 2006; Tarone, 2006; Rueda *et al.* 2010). Beef liver has been used in most of the laboratories for rearing flies of forensic importance but it leads to offensive odour and contamination. Therefore, there is need to develop artificial diet which is ideal and have no side effects. According to Clark *et al.* (2006) the blow fly *L. sericatna* larvae developed faster on pig than the tissues of cow and when reared on lungs and heart compared to liver. However, artificial diet powdered milk can cause a lower duration of larval stages in comparison to animal liver (Tachibana and Numata, 2001). According to Smith and Wall (1997) overcrowding of larvae can decrease growth rate and resulting in an under estimation of PMI. In general biological studies have tremendous importance in forensic science and biological studies of forensic insects are extremely needed for forensic science.

6 ECOLOGY OF FORENSIC INSECTS

INTRODUCTION

Forensic insects play a very crucial role in solving-problems related to murder, suicide, sexual molestation, child-neglect and abuse (Arutjunov, 1963). The environment, time of death of a person, road used and unknown place of dead bodies are detected by insects. Forensic insects develop on various vertebrates such as: mammals, birds, reptiles, amphibians, etc. The vertebrate carcasses are good source of food as they contain rich organic matter needed for development for many organisms, including insects. Insects in nature play a significant role in the decomposition of dead bodies of animals including man. The carrion insects such as: Dipterans and Coleopterans are attracted to the cadaver in a relative predictable sequence called as entomofauna succession or insect succession (Marchenko, 1988; Putman, 1983; Schoenly and Reid, 1987). This pattern of insect succession helps in post mortem interval (PMI) which further helps to solve murder mysteries.

Knowledge about species involved in corpse or carrion decomposition and the association of insects have tremendous value in forensic science. Each decomposition stage of the carcass has specific insects association. There are eight stages of carcass decomposition. Many insects are common on human and other vertebrate bodies for their development (Sathe and Jadav, 2013). Therefore, ecology of forensically important insects associated with carcasses of various animals from Kolhapur region has been studied.

Western Ghats of Maharashtra is located between 8°20′-20° 40′ N latitude and 73°-77° E longitude at an average elevation of 3900ft with about 2000-6000 mm rainfall. Western Ghats is biodiversity rich area of India but, under serious threat due to human interference in forest ecosystems. Blowflies (Diptera: Calliphoridae), flesh flies (Diptera: Sarcophagidae) and several beetles of families Histeridae, Cleridae, Meloidae, Dermestidae, etc., have significant value for solving forensic problems. Their role as carcass decomposer in forest and other ecosystems is also very crucial.

Biotic and abiotic factors have direct impact on population dynamics of flora and fauna. Extension tourism in forestry and changing lifestyle of humans lead criminal cases. The ecological diversity of Diptera is remarkable hence detecting its role in forensic science would be interesting. Therefore, altitudinal diversity of forensic insects has also a great relevance in protecting wild and human life and the data will be helpful for forensic science.

Review of literature indicates that ecology of forensic insects has been studied by several authors. Noteworthy amongst them refer to Senior White *et al.* (1940), James (1947), Putman (1977), Smith (1986), Greenberg (1991), Cross key and Lane (1993), Kurahashi and Thapa (1994), Stevens and Wall (1997), Smith and Wall (1997), Anderson (2001), Byrd and Castner (2001), Dadour *et al.* (2001), Kurahashi (2001), Kurahashi and Chowanadisai (2001), Tachibana and Numata (2001), Nandi (2004), Bharti and Singh (2003), Grassberger *et al.* (2003), Pitts and Wall (2004), Singh and Sidhu (2004, 2007), Kimberly (2005), Ronges (2005, 2009), Clark *et al.* (2006), Bharti (2009, 2012), Bharti and Kurahashi (2010), Higley and Haskel (2010), Shiravi *et al.* (2011), Vasconcelos *et al.* (2012), Sathe *et al.* (2013), Sathe and Jadav (2013,2014), Vasconcelos *et al.* (2013), Ghodake *et al.* (2014), Ghodake *et al.* (2014), Jadav and Sathe (2014, 2015), etc.

MATERIALS AND METHODS

Forensic insect samples were collected from carcasses of various animals such as: dog, rat and cow accidently died on the roadways. The insects were collected with the help of insect net and anesthetized and killed in the laboratory with chloroform and pinned with the help of entomological pins. The pinned insects were sufficiently dried (60°C) in drying chamber then viewed for morphological studies for identification with the help of compound microscope and appropriate literature citied under references. Ecological observations (seasonal abundance, distribution, sex ratio) of forensic insects were made during the years 2012-15 from Kolhapur, Radhanagari, Gaganbawada, Karveer, Shirol and Ajara covering most of the altitudinal and roadside spots of the district Kolhapur. The forensic insects were collected with the help of sweeping net from the carcasses. The carcasses of dog, cat, rat and buffalo were used in the present study. Collections were made weekly. After recording morphological features and identification, the insects were released in the environment from which they were collected.

Geographical and climatic data of study spots have been noted in the Table 6.1. and Fig. 6.1. Developmental aspects were accounted at field conditions by spot observations. Egg deposition time, egg hatching, larval stages and pupal developmental time were taken into account by spot observations. Sex ratio was counted within the insect groups collected on the carcasses and by counting actual number of males and females.

RESULTS

Blowflies, the blue bottles and green bottles which belong to the family Calliphoridae were small to large, robustly-build metallic blue green and covered with more or less with dusting. Our observations indicated that adults were vegetarians and frequently visited vegetation or flowers. They also visited excrement or decaying animals and plant matters. But, for larvae position/oviposition they were tremendously attracted to carcasses of animals including human cadavers. The maggots of blowflies were carnivorous or parasitic or omnivorous. They also played a role of scavengers by feeding on dung, garbage, carrion and feces. Larvae of some blowflies were parasitic on insects, snails, earthworms and mammals. Therefore, they have tremendous importance in medical, veterinary and forensic sciences.

Results recorded in Table 6.2 and 6.3 indicated that a total of 11 species of forensic insects belonging to the orders Diptera (12) and Coleoptera (4), Dactyoptera (1), Hymenoptera (2) and Anoplura (1) have been found associated with carcasses of dog, cat, rat and buffalo at Kolhapur (Table 6.2). Flesh flies appeared very first on all carcasses selected for the present study at a moist stage before 6 hours for egg laying, second arrived insects were blow flies. They occurred before 24 hours and beetles appeared at active stage and the advanced stages of decomposition of carcasses. They were found feeding on the muscles attached to the bones and most interior parts. The maggots of flies were related to feeding on muscles of superficial as well as various organs and interior part of the carcass. The development of forensic insects on carcasses of dog has been shown in Table 6.3.

Results recorded in Table 6.2 indicated that a total of 12 species of blow flies, 07 species of sarcophagids and 04 species of beetles were prevalent in Kolhapur district. The dominant order of insects prevalent in Kolhapur region was Diptera followed by Coleoptera, Hymenoptera, Dactyoptera and Anapleura.

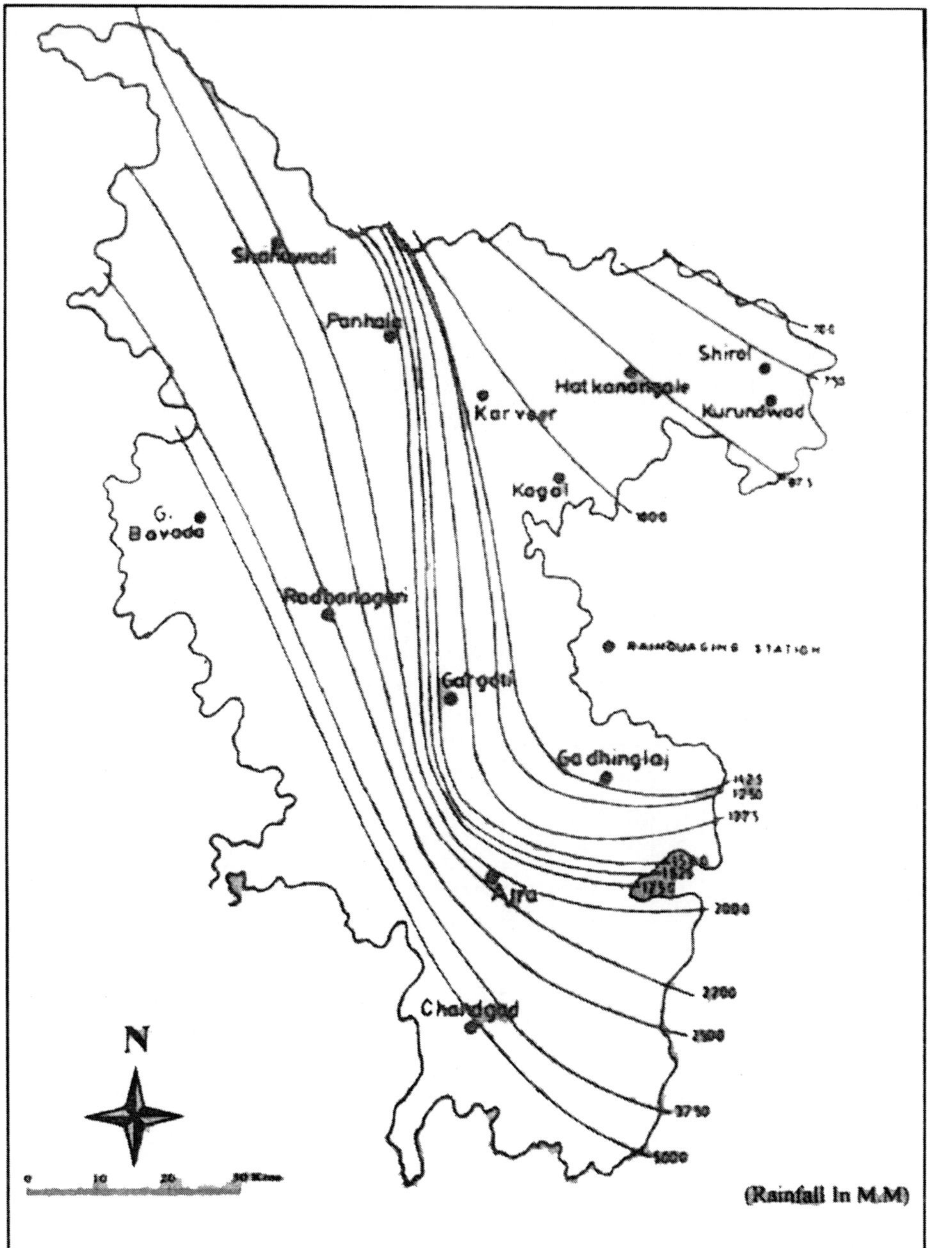

Fig. 6.1: **Annual Rainfall form Kolhapur District**

Table 6.1: Geographical and Climatic Conditions of Kolhapur District (Study Spots)

SL. No.	Place	Altitude (m)	Latitude (°N)	Longitude (°E)	Temperature (°C)	Humidity (%)	Rainfall (mm)
1.	Kolhapur	545.6	16.42	74.16	10-40	65-87	1000-1025
2.	Radhanagari	585.0	16.41	73.99	10-38	67-90	2500
3.	Gaganbawada	900	16.545	73.83	10-32	64-94	5000-6000
4.	Ajara	660	16.12	14.02	12-38	80-90	2000-2700
5.	Shirol	545.00	16.44	74.36	10-40	75-80	750

Table 6.2: Occurrence and Distribution of Forensic insects from Kolhapur District on Various Animal Carcasses

Sl. No.	Carcass				Locality	Occurrence	Species	Order	Family
	Dog	Cat	Rat	Buffalo					
1.	+	+	+	+	Kolhapur	Common	*Chrysomya megacephala* (Fab.)	Diptera	Calliphoridae
	+	+	+	+		Common	*Chrysomya rufifacies* (Macquart)	Diptera	Calliphoridae
	+	-	+	-		Common	*Chrysomya indica* Nandi	Diptera	Calliphoridae
	+	+	+	+		Common	*Chrysomya chain* Kurahashi	Diptera	Calliphoridae
	+	-	+	-		Common	*Lucilia ampullaceal* Villeneuve	Diptera	Calliphoridae
	+	-	+	-		Common	*Lucilia papuensis* Macquart	Diptera	Calliphoridae
	+	-	+	+		Common	*Lucilia porphyrina* (Walker)	Diptera	Calliphoridae
	+	+	+	-		Rare	*Calliphora erythrocephala* (Meigen)	Diptera	Calliphoridae
	+	-	+	+		Common	*Sarcophaga josephi* Buttcher	Diptera	Sarcophagidae
	+	-	+	+		Common	*Sarcophaga udhgiriensis* sp. nov.	Diptera	Sarcophagidae
	+	+	-	+		Common	*Sarcophaga orientalis* Parker	Diptera	Sarcophagidae
	+	+	-	-		Common	*Piophila sp.*	Diptera	Piophoridae
	+	+	+	-		Common	*Creophilis sp.*	Coleoptera	Staphylinidae
	+	-	-	+		Common	*Necrophila rufithorax* (Wied.)	Coleoptera	Silphidae
	+	-	-	-		Common	*Necrobia rufipes* (De Geer)	Coleoptera	Cleridae
	+	+	+	+		Common	*Saprinus splendens* (Paykull)	Coleoptera	Histeridae
	-	-	-	-		Common	*Periplaneta americana* (Linnaeus)	Dictyoptera	Blattidae

Contd...

Sl. No.	Carcass				Locality	Occurrence	Species	Order	Family
	Dog	Cat	Rat	Buffalo					
	-	-	-	-		Common	*Pediculus humanus* De Geer	Anapluera	Pediculidae
	+	+	+	+		Common	*Campotonotus compressus*	Hymeno-	Formicidae
	-	-	+	-		Common	Hymenopteran parasitoid	ptera	——
2.	+	+	+	+	Radhanagari	Common	*Chrysomya megacephala* (Fab.)	Diptera	Calliphoridae
	+	+	+	+		Common	*Chrysomya rufifacies* (Macquart)	Diptera	Calliphoridae
	+	+	+	+		Common	*Chrysomya nigricpes* (Wied.)	Diptera	Calliphoridae
	+	-	-	+		Common	*Chrysomya chani* Kurahashi	Diptera	Calliphoridae
	+	-	-	+		Common	*Lucilia ampullacea* Villeneuve	Diptera	Calliphoridae
	+	+	-	+		Common	*Lucilia papuensis* Macquart	Diptera	Calliphoridae
	+	-	+	+		Common	*Lucilia sericata* (Meigen)	Diptera	Calliphoridae
	-	-	-	+		Rare	*Calliphora erythrocephala* (Meigen)	Diptera	Calliphoridae
	+	+	-	+		Common	*Sarcophaga sera* Rohd.	Diptera	Sarcophagidae
	+	+	-	+		Common	*Sarcophaga pes-helicis* Sen.-White	Diptera	Sarcophagidae
	+	+	-	+		Common	*Piophila sp.*	Diptera	Piophilidae
	+	-	-	-		Rare	*Necrobia rufipes* (De Geer)	Coleoptera	Cleridae
	-	-	-	-		Common	*Periplaneta americana* (Linnaeus)	Dictyoptera	Blattidae
	-	-	-	-		Common	*Pediculus humanus capitis* De Geer	Anopluera	Pediculidae
	-	-	+	+		Common	*Campotonotus compressus*	Hymenoptera	Formicidae
3.	+	+	+	+	Gaganbavda	Common	*Chrysomya megacephala* (Fab.)	Diptera	Calliphoridae
	+	+	+	+		Common	*Chrysomya rufifacies* (Macquart)	Diptera	Calliphoridae

Contd...

Sl. No.	Carcass				Locality	Occurrence	Species	Order	Family
	Dog	Cat	Rat	Buffalo					
	+	-	-	-		Rare	*Chrysomya villenuevi* Patt.	Diptera	Calliphoridae
	+	+	+	+		Common	*Chrysomya nigricpes* (Wied.)	Diptera	Calliphoridae
	+	-	+	-		Common	*Lucilia ampullaceal* Villeneuve	Diptera	Calliphoridae
	-	+	+	+		Common	*Lucilia illustris* (Meigen)	Diptera	Calliphoridae
	+	+	-	-		Common	*Sarcophaga baranossi* Sen.-White	Diptera	Sarcophagidae
	+	+	+	+		Common	*Sarcophaga udhgiriensis* sp nov	Diptera	Sarcophagidae
	+	+	+	+		Common	*Piophila sp.*	Diptera	Piophilidae
	+	-	-	-		Common	*Necrobia rufipes* (De Geer)	Coleoptera	Cleridae
	+	-	-	+		Common	*Saprinus splendens* (Paykull)	Coleoptera	Histeridae
	-	-	-	-		Common	*Periplaneta americana* (Linnaeus)	Dactyoptera	Blattidae
	-	-	-	-		Common	*Pediculus humanus capitis*	Anapleura	Pediculidae
	-	-	+	+		Common	De Geer *Campotonotus compressus*	Hymenoptera	Formicidae
4.	+	+	+	+	Ajra	Common	*Chrysomya megacephala* (Fab.)	Diptera	Calliphoridae
	+	+	+	+		Common	*Chrysomya nigripes* (Wied.)	Diptera	Calliphoridae
	+	+	-	+		Common	*Chrysomya ruffacies* (Macquart)	Diptera	Calliphoridae
	-	+	+	+		Common	*Lucilia sericata* (Meigen)	Diptera	Calliphoridae
	+	+	-	+		Common	*Lucilia cuprina* (Wied.)	Diptera	Calliphoridae
	+	+	+	+		Common	*Sarcophaga josephi* Buttcher	Diptera	Sarcophagidae
	+	-	+	+		Common	*Sarcophaga sera* Rohd.	Diptera	Sarcophagidae
	+	+	+	+		Common	*Piophila sp.*	Diptera	Piophilidae
	+	+	+	-		Common	*Saprinus splendens* (Paykull)	Coleoptera	Histeridae
	-	-	-	-		Common	*Periplaneta americana* (Linnaeus)	Dactyoptera	Blattidae

Contd...

Sl. No.	Carcass				Locality	Occurrence	Species	Order	Family
	Dog	Cat	Rat	Buffalo					
	-	-	-	-		Common	*Pediculus humanus capitis* De Geer	Anapleura	Pediculidae
	-	-	+	+		Common	*Campotonotus compressus*	Hymenoptera	Formicidae
5.	+	+	+	+	Shirol	Common	*Chrysomya megacephala* (Fab.)	Diptera	Calliphoridae
	+	+	+	+		Common	*Chrysomya rufifacies* (Macquart)	Diptera	Calliphoridae
	+	-	+	+		Common	*Chrysomya indica* Nandi	Diptera	Calliphoridae
	+	+	-	-		Common	*Chrysomya chani* Kurahashi	Diptera	Calliphoridae
	-	+	+	+		Common	*Calliphora erythrocephala*(Meigen)	Diptera	Calliphoridae
	+	-	+	+		Common	*Sarcophaga josephi* Buttcher	Diptera	Sarcophagidae
	+	-	+	+		Common	*Sarcophaga orientalis* Parker	Diptera	Sarcophagidae
	+	+	+	+		Common	*Piophila sp.*	Diptera	Piophilidae
	+	-	+	-		Common	*Necrobia rufipes* (De Geer)	Coleoptera	Cleridae
	+	-	+	+		Common	*Saprinus splendens* (Paykull)	Coleoptera	Histeridae
	-	-	-	-		Common	*Periplaneta americana* (Linnaeus)	Dactyoptera	Blattidae
	-	-	-	-		Common	*Pediculus humanus* De Geer	Anapluera	Pediculidae
	-	-	+	+		Common	*Campotonotus compressus*	Hymenoptera	Formicidae

Table 6.3: Development of Forensic Insects on Carcasses of Dog

Sl. No.	Species	Duration (In days)
1.	*S. lineatocollis*	14.00
2.	*S. calcitrans*	13.5
3.	*C. rufifacies*	10.00
4.	*L. sericata*	10.00
5.	*C. vicina*	8.50
6.	*N. rufithorax*	15
7.	*Hister sp.*	17.5
8.	*D. maculatus*	18
9.	*N. rufipes*	16-18

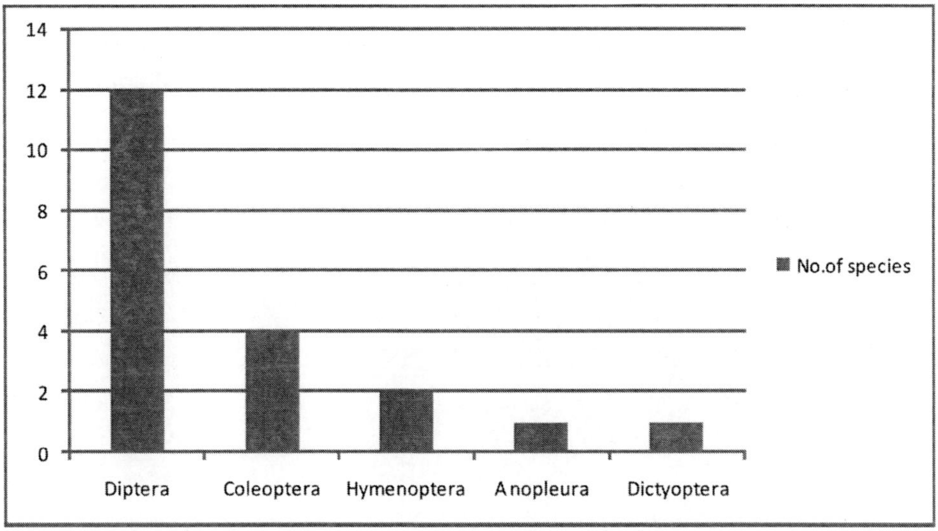

Fig. 6.2: **Abundance of forensic insects in Kolhapur district**

Discussion

Blow flies (Diptera: Calliphoridae), the green bottles and the blue bottles are important component of forensic science. The blue bottles *Calliphora* occur commonly around houses in search of breeding material and food and attracted to meat, carrion, fecal matter and dead animals for egg laying and to cheese for food. The genus *Chrysomya* includes green bottles of large size and metallic green color and cause myiasis in human and other animals in India. This genus is reported from India, Africa, Philippines, Celebes and New Guinea. *Lucilia* species are also known as green bottles and are metallic,

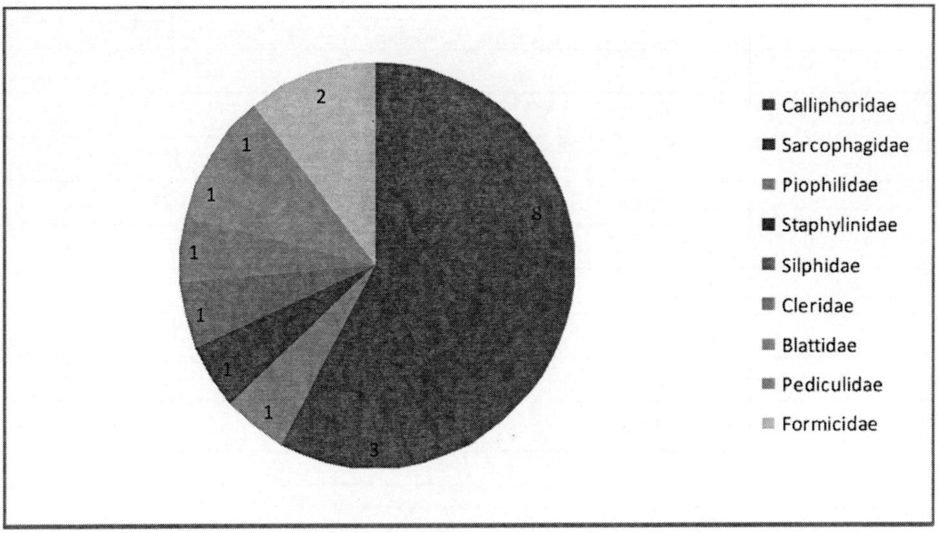

Fig. 6.3: **Abundance of forensic insects on carcasses in Kolhapur**

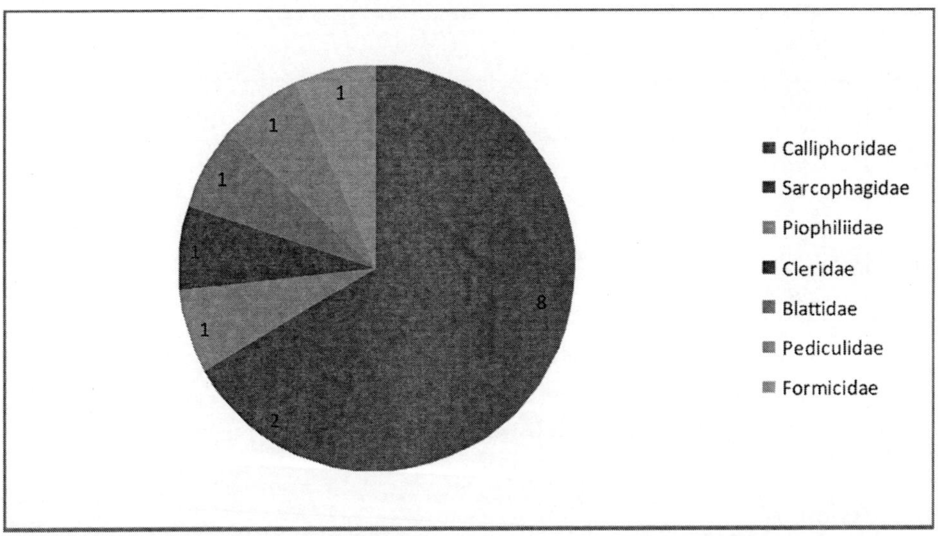

Fig. 6.4: **Abundance of forensic insects on carcasses in Radhanagari**

shining green but smaller and less bristly than *Calliphora*. The larvae of *Lucilia* infect wounds and body cavities in man and some attacks sheep in India. Western Ghats is one of 18 hot spots of the world for conservation and protection of biodiversity and visualized as gene rich area of India (Jadav and Sathe, 2015). Therefore, reporting forensic insects from Western Ghats is essential part of forensic science.

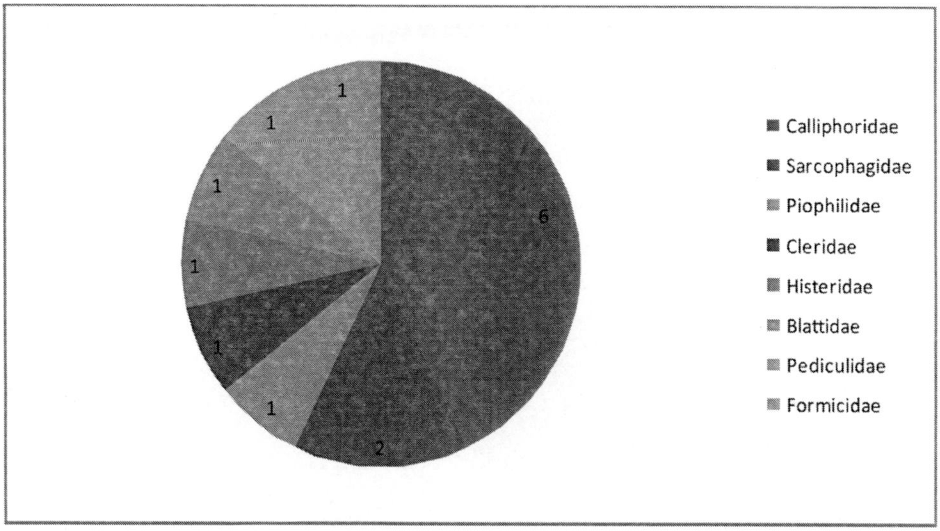

Fig. 6.5: **Abundance of forensic insects on carcasses in Gaganbavada**

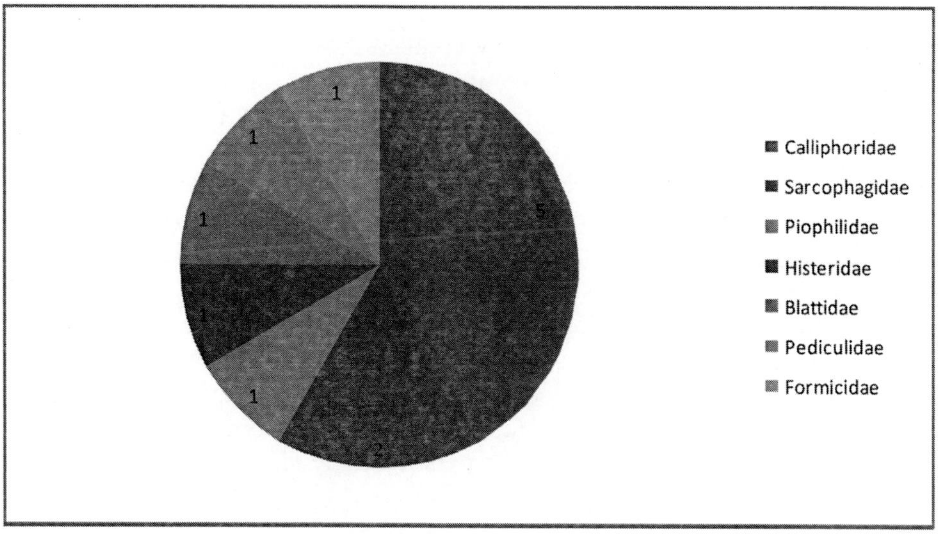

Fig. 6.6: **Abundance of forensic insects on carcasses in Ajara**

Vasconcelos *et al*. (2012) provided first check-list of forensically important dipteran species in a rainforest environment in North eastern Brazil, a region exposed to high rates of homicides. They used a decomposing pig *Susscrofa* L. (Artiodacetyla: Suidae) carcass as a model and adult flies were collected immediately after death in the early stages of carcass decomposition. To confirm actual colonization of the carcass, insects that completed their

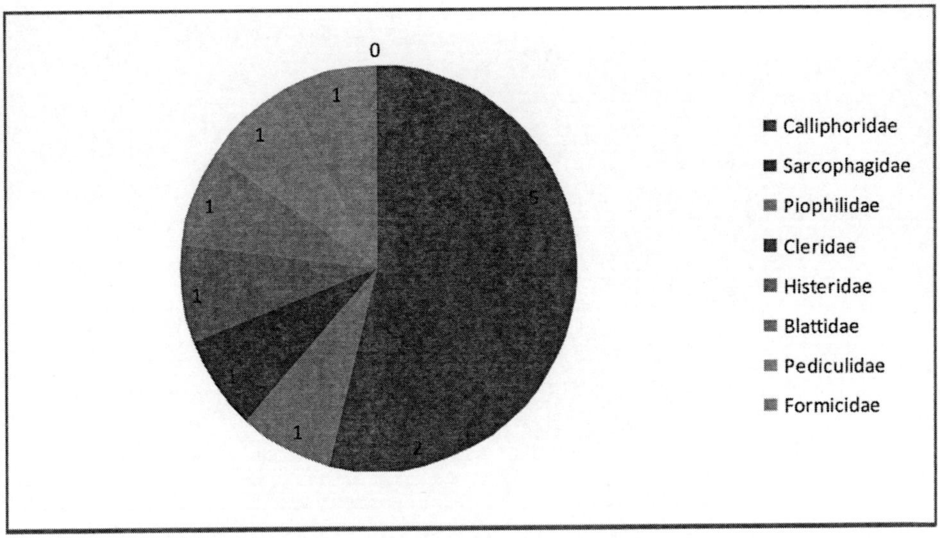

Fig. 6.7: **Abundance of forensic insects on carcasses in Shirol**

larval development on the resource were also collected and reared until the adult stage. They noted 28 species of seven families of order Diptera with necrophagus habits within few minutes after death. Out of 28 species, 11 have completed their larval development on carcass. The majority of individuals emerged from larvae collected at the dry stage of decomposition. *Hemilucilia segmentaria* Fab. (Calliphoridae), *H. semidiaphana* (Rondani) and *Ophyra chalcoguster* (Wied.) (Muscidae) were the dominant species among the colonizers. During the six months sampled, a total of 3,262 flies were collected from the ten collection sites. The surveys in Muang Ubon Ratchathani and Warinchamrap districts yielded a total of 2,257 and 1,005 flies, respectively. The dominant species captured was the blow fly, *Chrysomya megacephala* (Fabricius), which ranked first in prevalence at all the collection sites, followed by *Musca domestica* L. (Chaiwong *et al*. 2012).

Sathe *et al*. (2013) recorded a total of 25 species of dipterous forensic insects from Kolhapur region, India. Similarly, Sathe and Jadav (2014) studied the diversity and occurrence of Sarcophagids and reported 16 species from Kolhapur District, India. Dipterous flies play an important role in decomposing the carcasses (Ghodake *et al*. 2014; Sathe and Jadav, 2014). Different species of Calliphorids have adapted to different feeding habits over the years for their survival and broadly divided as saprophages, facultative parasites like: *C. megacephala* and *Lucilia sericata* Meigen and obligate parasites causing myiasis in man and other animals like: *Chrysomya bezziana* (Villeneuve). They were also adapted to various ecological niches (Stevens and Walls, 1997).

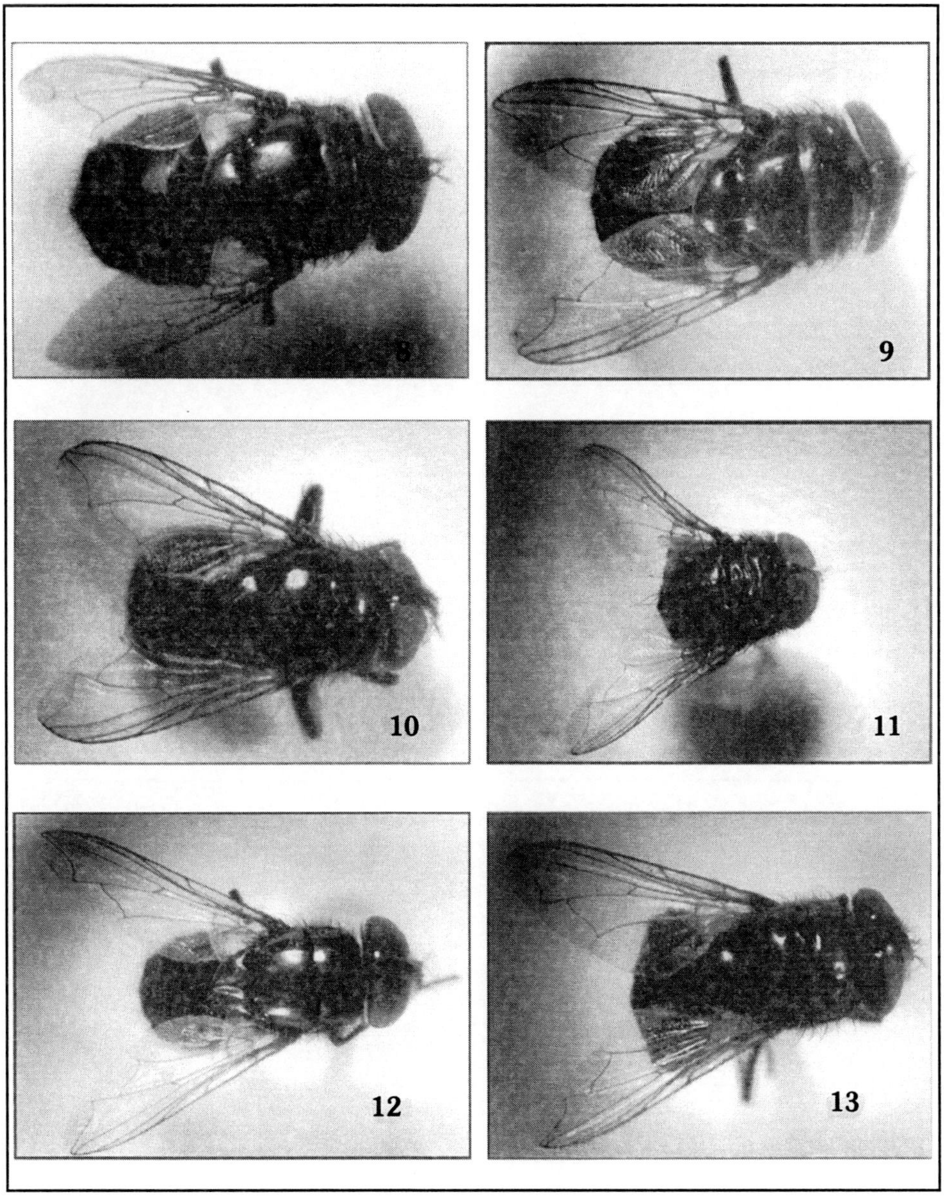

Plate - I: Blowflies (8-13) Fig. 6.8: ***C.rufifacies,*** Fig. 6.9: ***C. megacephala,*** Fig. 6.10: ***C.villeneuve,*** Fig. 6.11: ***C.chani,*** Fig. 6.12: ***C.nigrepes,*** Fig. 6.13: ***Lucillia Sp.***

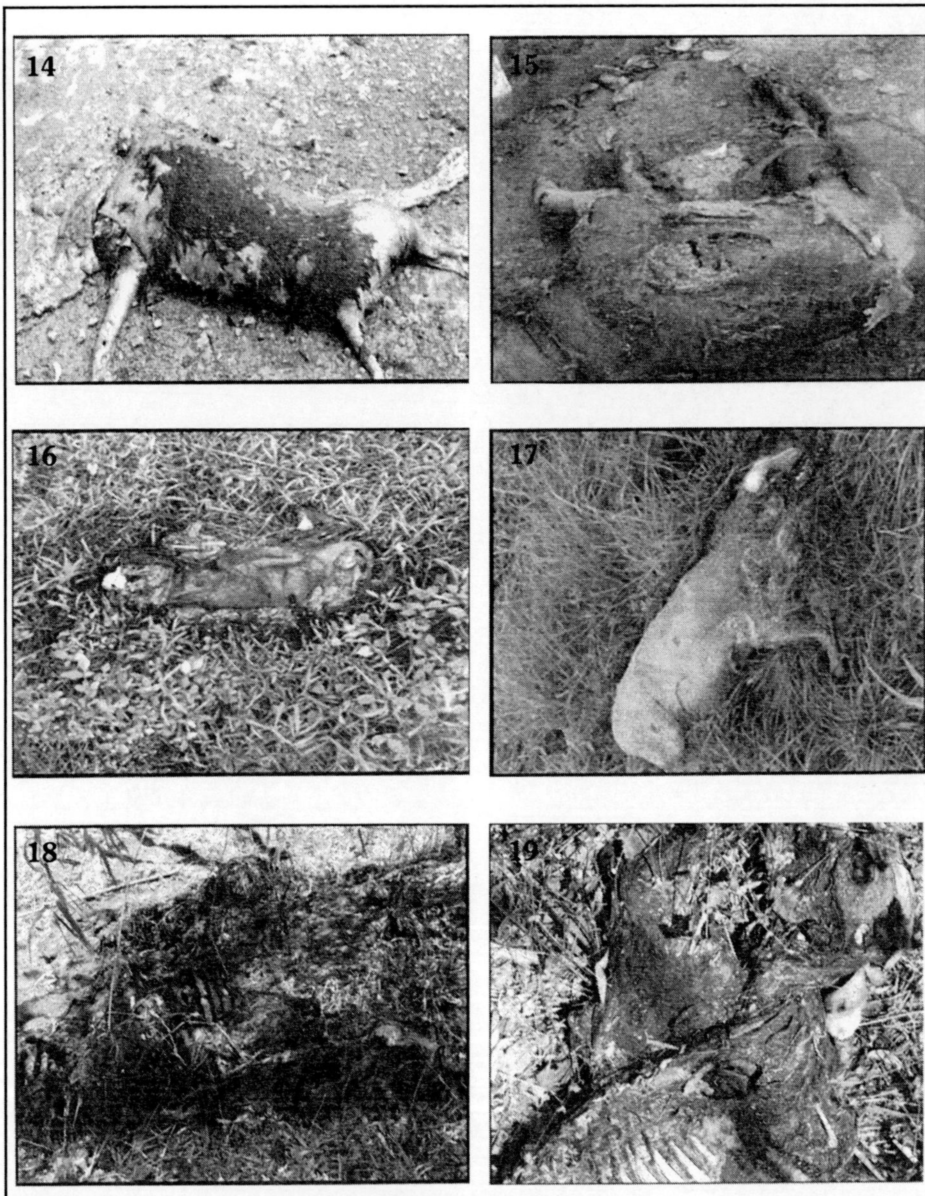

Plate - II: Carcasses of Animals at Different Study Spots (14-19)
Fig. 6.14: ***Carcass of dog at Gaganbavda,*** Fig. 6.15: ***Carcass of Dog at Kagal (Kolhapur),*** Fig. 6.16: ***Carcass of Dog at Kolhapur,*** Fig. 6.17: ***Carcass of dog at Katyani (Kolhapur),*** Fig. 6.18: ***Carcass of Buffala at Radhanagari,*** Fig. 6.19: ***Carcass of calf (buffalo) at Radhanagari***

According to Shiravi *et al.* (2011) the developmental rates in *Chrysomya albiceps* (Wiedmann) and *L. sericata* were highly different in terms of accumulation of degree days required than that of the flesh fly *Sarcophaga sp.* They reported that the speed of development in the flesh fly was slower than blowflies. At 28°C the total developmental time from egg to adult was 13-19 days in *Sarcophaga sp.*, while, Jadav and Sathe (2014) reported 13-15 days and 7-19 days for the development of flesh flies and blow flies respectively.

According to Hall and Doisy (1993) the amount of time after death affected the structure of the assemblage of insects attracted to a carcass, a feature that will have direct implications on the accuracy of the biological information available to the forensic entomologist. The time and arrival of insect colonies can be estimated in dead body (Greenberg, 1991). Insect life cycle begins within minutes of death which act as precise clock. The growth of insect larvae that feed upon the victim and the succession of carrion arthropod species found in body are helpful for minimum and maximum estimates of post mortem mechanisms in medical-forensic science. According to Kashyap and Pillai (1989) forensic entomology is highly accurate from 72 hours after death. Coleopterans were second decomposers and became most important forensic indicators during later stages of decomposition of carcass on dog. Besides ecological importance in decomposition, the forensic insects particularly blowflies representing important tool in criminal investigations serving as a biological clock in measuring the time since death for weeks or even for months. The necrophagus species and their predators and parasites were the important insects to be attracted to the body immediately after death even within minutes (Smith, 1986).

According to Lord and Burger (1983) forensic insect specimens should be treated as physical evidence like: blood-strains, hair, finger prints or any other biological material. All the insect specimens of different shape and size and from everywhere on and around the corpse should be preserved in vials containing 70-95 per cent ethanol so that their morphological and molecular identification is made easy. According to Sharma (2008) forensic insects provide very useful information not only in a death investigation including time since death, season of death, geographical location of death, movement or storage of the remains after death, time of decapitation or dismemberment, submersion interval, use of damage but even more in linking a suspect to the scene of crime, in child neglect and sexual molestations or identification of suspects. Although there is a specificity of certain forensic insects with the host species, many forensic insects are common on majority of the vertebrate carcasses. Therefore, the present work would be the base line data for forensic insects probably associated with even human beings.

As like dipterous flies, coleopterous beetles also play an important role in decomposition of carcasses. They appear on the active and advanced stages of decomposition (Sathe and Jadav, 2013). Putman (1977) studied the important coleopteran species associated with carcasses as second decomposers which refer to *Dermestes maculates* (De Geer) (Dermestidae), *Oxyletrum disciolle* (Zett) (Silphidae), *Necrobia rufipes* (Fabricius) (Cleridae), *Trox* sp. (Troxidae) and *Hister* sp. (Histeridae). These species used carcasses simply for their life cycle, food and shelter. The adults and larvae of coleopterans were dominated and responsible for maximum consumption of terrestrial carrion.

Szymon *et al.* (2008) recorded insect succession and pig carrion decomposition in pine, hornbean oak forests and alder forest in Western Poland at the end of summer and beginning of fall, 2005. They noted 5 stages of decomposition namely: fresh, bloated, active decay, advanced decay and remains stage. Zahid *et al.* (2013) studied the coleopterous species associated with *C. domesticus* cadaver in tropical region of Mavdan, Pakistan. They collected *D. maculates*, *Hister* sp., *Trox*sp. and *N. rufipes*. *Hister* sp., adults and larvae dominated the later stages of decomposition. The temperature (28.3±1.8 – 40.4±1.7) was found to affect coleopteran adults, larvae and rate of decomposition of *C. domestics* during the observation period. The highest decomposition rate was observed in the alder forest than in the pine oak forest. Similarity, in carrion fauna was found in each forest. The beetles recorded from both of the forests were hairy rove beetles, *Thanatophilus rugosus* (Linnaeus) (Silphidae), *Creophilus maxillosus* (Linnaeus) (Staphylinidae), rove beetles, *Oxypoda acuminate* (Stephens) (Staphylinidae), *Omalium rivulare* (Paykull) (Staphylinidae) and *Philonthus* sp. (Stephen) (Staphylinidae).

Forensic insect identification based on genetic examination such as: DNA analysis is an option. DNA of human blood can be successfully extracted from carrion blood-feeding insect specimen collected from a crime scene which might have fed on the cadaver. The presence of DNA of suspect within the insects at a known location within a definable period of time may establish a link between the victim and the crime. A case has been reported where the DNA recovered from the crime scene matched to that of murder suspect (Sumodan, 2002). Carvalho *et al.* (2000) studied insect succession on carcasses in Brazil. They reported 3 species belonging to 3 families *i.e. D. maculates* and *O. disciolle* (Brullé), were belonging to families of Dermestidae and Silphidae, respectively and *N. rufipes* to family Cleridae. The adults and larvae of *D. maculates* were dominated in later stages of decomposition. Within minutes of death, forensic insects were able to locate the dead body through the sense of smell (Rawant *et al.* 2014). Flies, mainly flesh flies and blow flies arrived first at the decomposing corpse. The female fly deposited eggs (Calliphorid flies) or larvae (Sarcophagids flies) on open wound or natural orifices, such as: nose, mouth and anus of the corpse. These larvae then fed on the decaying corpse. Other insects such as: beetles, ants, moths and butterflies arrived later and decomposed the corpse (Rawant *et al.* 2014).

According to Rawant *et al.* (2014) flies (Diptera) were often first on the scene. They preferred a moist corpse for the maggots to feed on, as such a corpse was easier for them to chew. The most important insects and families were: blow flies (Calliphoridae), flesh flies (Sarcophagidae), house flies (Muscidae), cheese flies (Piophilidae), coffin flies (Phoridae), lesser corpse flies (Sphaeroceridae), lesser house flies (Fanniidae), black scavenger flies (Sepsidae), sun flies (Heleomyzidae) and black soldier fly (Stratiomyidae). These mostly break down fatty and proteinaceous part of the dead body. Various lipasases, proteases and peptidases found in their saliva were mostly responsible for decomposition. Beetles (Coleoptera) were generally found on the corpse when it was more decomposed. In drier conditions, the beetles were replaced by moth flies (Psychodidae). Rove beetles (Staphylinidae), hister beetles (Histeridae), carrion beetles (Silphidae), ham beetles (Cleridae), carcass beetles (Trogidae), skin/hide beetles (Dermestidae) were important in the final stages of decomposition of a carcass. Hide beetles were the only beetle with the enzymes necessary for breaking down keratin, a protein component of hair. According to Rawat *et al.* (2014) many mites were also fed on a corpse. Macrochele mites were common in the early stages of decomposition, while, Tyroglyphidae and Oribatidae mites (Rostrozetes) fed on dry skin in the later stages of decomposition. Necrophorus beetles carried on their bodies the mite *Poecilochirus* which fed on fly eggs. Clothes-moths (Tineidae) were feeding on mammalian hair during their larval stages and may forage on any hair that remains. They were amongst the final animals contributing to the decomposition of a corpse. In general, it is concluded that the forensic insects play very important role in judicial matter by providing evidences with their presence and such evidences should be considered as valid proof. However, the forensic entomology is still under developed in several countries including India. The present work will add great relevance in understanding forensic entomology of Kolhapur region, India.

According to Amendt *et al.* (2007) distribution of eggs or larvae (maggots) on a baby indicate presence of a wound from gunshot or stabbing. The insects found on the body can suggest that whether the body was moved from initial location. In cases of neglect or abuse, where a living person has become infested by insects (myiasis), ageing of the insects can indicate the period of mistreatment. The toxins present in the dead body can be detected with the help of insects feeding on carcass by critical analysis. DNA sequencing of dead person can also be obtained by insects feeding on the dead body.

Thus, the forensic entomology can assist in cases of wild life poaching and illegal importation of animal parts and sourcing of illegal plant material such as: cannabis, by identifying the origin of any insects present.

Forensic insects also play an important role in detecting food contamination wherein insects indicate when and where the food may spoil, either deliberately or through negligence.

Forensic insects and data preservation have tremendous importance in court as part of event evidence through insects. Therefore, correct and scientific protocols of methods of insect collection and data collection have tremendous importance otherwise insects may get spoiled. Insects like: dipterous flies, coleopterous beetles and hymenopterous wasps should be collected by insect net and dried sufficiently in drying chamber at 60°C and adult insects should be pinned properly. Dipterous insects should be pinned from ventral side from mesothorax that pin should not be emerged from the dorsal side intact, pinning should not be made from dorsal side so that the chaetotaxy of the insect should not damage as it is extremely essential for running key for identification of insects. However, forensic hymenopterous insects should be pinned from dorsal side from mesothorax (Sathe, 2005).

The corpses have eight decomposing stages and the insects have specificity with the decomposing stages. Dipterous insects like: flesh flies, blowflies, house flies, cheese skipper flies, coffin flies, lesser corpse flies, sun flies, scavenger flies, soldier flies, etc., appeared first on the corpse which was responsible for breaking down fatty and proteinous part of the dead body (Rawat *et al.* 2014). Second arrivals on corpse were beetles. The beetles associated at second stage of decomposition refer to rove beetles, hister beetles, carrion beetles, ham beetles and carcass beetles. The skin or hide beetles played important role in the final stages of decomposition of corpse (Rawat *et al.* 2014). While, lepidopterous larvae of clothes moth were associated with the dead body for feeding on the hairs. Thus, insects play a very crucial role in the ecological recycling of carcass and obtaining clues in crime detection such as: time of death, region of death occurred, transportation ways used, toxic materials responsible for death, etc.

Sasha *et al.* (2009) examined the insect succession variations on the decomposing remains in two areas, bush land and agriculture of Western Australia. They reported 3 beetles involved in decomposition of carcass which refer to *Ptomaphila lacrymosa* (Schreibers) (Silphidae), *Omorgus tatei* (Blackburn) (Trogidae) and *Helea castor* (Pascoe) (Tenebrionidae). According to Vasconcelos *et al.* (2013) two Calliphorids namely: *Hemilucillia segmentaria* (Fabricius) and *H. semidiaphana* (Rondani) were dominant in rain forest fragment on animal carcasses in Brazil. Besides Calliphoridae and Sarcophagidae species, forensically important families such as: Phoridae, Anthomyidae and Fannidae were also registered from rain forest of Brazil. *Lucillia sericata* (Meigen) played significant role in human medicine. Its larvae were used for healing chronic injuries that donor respond to conventional treatments in case of ulcers and gangrenous or necrotic tissues (Gupta, 2008). The present work is very good baseline data for forensic science for Kolhapur region for protecting wildlife and human life.

Jadav and Sathe (2014) studied the altitudinal diversity of blowflies of Western Ghats. They reported 19 species of blow flies have been reported from the selected spots of Western Ghats (Maharashtra) belonging to the genera *Chrysomya, Lucilia* and *Calliphora*. The genus Chrysomya was represented by 6 species namely: *Chrysomyamegacephala, C. indica, C. bazziana, C. rufifacies, C. nigripes* and *C. marginalis* and the genus *Lucilia* by nine species, *Lucilia sericata, L. cuprina, L. vicina, L. papuensis, L. ampullacea, L. illustris, L. porphyrina, L. andrewsi* and *L. bazini* while, the genus *Calliphora* represented by only four species *viz; Calliphora vicina, C. erythrocephala, C. vomitono* and *C. bazini*. In Kolhapur city, the genera *Lucilia, Chrysomya and Calliphora* were common with a total of seven species. Gaganbawda, the highest altitude spot showed *Calliphora, Chrysomya* and *Lucilia* genera with 1, 3 and 2 species respectively. While the Sindhudurg, attitudinally lowest spot showed 13 species of blow flies belonging to the genera *Chrysomya, Lucilia* and *Calliphora* with 5, 6 and 2 species respectively. Their results indicated that the blow flies population was increased during the monsoon season than the winter and summer season and diversity of blow flies was found decreased with increase in altitude in the Western Ghats. It was noted that in almost every spot blowflies gathered on meat piece within half an hour expect Chrysomya which appeared 3 hours. They reported that number of attracted blowflies was decreased with increase of altitude. The blowflies were also found increased in number on goat meat after 30 minutes of exposure. In general, qualitative and quantitative diversity of blowflies were more in monsoon than winter and summer. The outcome of faunal turn over analysis clearly indicated that assemblage at 545 m and 585 m share almost 71.42 per cent of their fauna in common. Also elevation of 900 m shares 70.70 per cent of its assemblage with 585 m. Similarly, assemblage at 42 m and 22 m share about 40 per cent of their fauna in common.

Life cycle duration of *C. erythrocephala* and *L. sericata* from egg to adult indicated that they completed their life cycle on different carcasses (dog, cat and buffalo) within the range of 9 days to 11 days at 27 ± 1°C, 70-80 per cent and 12 hr photoperiod in the laboratory. There was not much difference in developmental life stages duration in both the species even on different carcasses. The life cycle of blow flies included four distinct stages *viz;* egg larva, pupa and imago. In the maggot stage 3 instars were noted. The flies deposited their eggs directly on carcasses. The eggs were elongated, the larvae were whitish opaque, legless and tapered towards anterior side and broader towards posterior side and were further characterized by number of respiratory slits at posterior end. The third instar was lasted longer than others on carcasses and found feeding on host tissues. The pupal duration was about half the length of the total development.

According to Stevens and Walls (1997) different species of Calliphorids have adapted to different feeding habits over the years for their survival and broadly divided as saprophages, facultative parasites like: *Chrysomya megacephala* and *Lucilia sericata* and obligate parasites causing myiasis in man and other animals like: *Chrysomya bezziana*. They were also adapted to various ecological niches.

Bharti (2012) studied altitudinal diversity of forensically important blow flies from Himalaya on decaying carcasses. A total of 14 species belonging to the genera *Calliphora, Chrysomya* and *Lucilia* have been reported. Out of 14 species, 6 were from the genus *Chrysomya,* 2 from the genus *Calliphora* while 6 were from the genus *Lucilia*. Bharti (2014) further reported that at an elevation of 350 m (Shivalik range of Himalaya), a total of five species namely: *C. megacephala, C. rufifacies, L. porphyrina, L. papuensis* and *L. ampullaceal* were present on the carcass. *C. megacephala* and *L. papuensis* were the most abundant species at this elevation. At 970 m also 5 species have been recorded (*C. megacephala, C. rufifacies, C. nigripes, L. illustris* and *L. ampullacea*). These species were found feeding and egg laying on the carcass. At this elevation, the fresh and bloating stages of decomposition of carcass were dominated by all 3 species of *Chrysomya* while, during the decay stage *C. nigripes* was most abundant. She reported maximum diversity of blow flies at an elevation of 2057m. A total of 8 species of blow flies were collected from cow carcass. Here *C. megacephala* and *L. sericata* were most abundant. Additional species occurred at this elevation were *C. albiceps, C. pinguis, C. villeneuvi, L. sericata* and *L. cuprina* and also *Calliphora vicina*. However, at an elevation of 2511 m only 3 species namely: *C. villeneuvi, Calliphora vicina* and *Calliphora vomitoria* were present. With increase in altitude there was a marked decrease in faunal diversity. Qualitative faunal diversity was different at different spots. The reason for maximum diversity of blow flies at Sindhudurg may be due to availability of more diverse host carcasses since it is a sea coastal spot (Jadav and Sathe, 2014).

Vasconcellos *et al.* (2013) provided first check-list of forensically important dipteran species in a rainforest environment in North eastern Brazil, a region exposed to high rates of homicides. They used a decomposing pig, *Susscrofa* L. (Artiodacetyla: Suidae), carcass as a model and adult flies were collected immediately after death and in the early stages of carcass decomposition. To confirm actual colonization of the carcass, insects that completed their larval development on the resource were also collected and reared until adult stage. They noted 28 species of seven families of order Diptera with necrophagus habits within few minutes after death. Out of 28 species, 11 have completed their larval development on carcass.

The majority of individuals emerged from larvae collected at the dry stage of decomposition. *Hemilucilia segmentaria* Fab. (Calliphoridae), *H. semidiaphana* (Rondani) and *Ophyra chalcoguster* (Wied.) (Muscidae) were the dominant species among the colonizers. According to Jadav and Sathe, 2014 the dominant species found in the Western Ghats was *Chrysomya megacephala*. However, the genus *Lucilia* represented maximum 6 species in the region with altitudinal specificity. At an elevation of 22 m Sindhudurg represented 6 species of *Lucilia and 5 species of Chysomya.* Vasconcelos *et al.* (2013) reported in total, 153 insects from 14 families in the first 3 hours after the death. This included species of Phoridae 24.2 per cent, Sarophagidae 18.3 per cent, Piophilidae 10.5 per cent, Calliphoridae 10.5 per cent, Fanniidae 8.5 per cent, Chloropidae 6.5 per cent, Muscidae 4.6 per cent and Dixidae 4.6 per cent while other families were in smaller proportions. The present study was pinpointed for the single family Calliphoridae. However, reporting other families from this region will be of great interest in future. Determination of post mortem interval (PMI) or the time between death and the discovery of the corpse is the most important application of forensic entomology. Flies belong to the families Calliphoridae (blow flies) and Sarcophagidae (flesh flies) are often the first insects to arrive on a corpse where their larvae feed and breed effectively (James, 1947; Higley and Haskell, 2010).

Developmental rates of flies are frequently used to estimate PMI in homicide investigations in the first few weeks after death. The development of immature insects is climate or temperature dependent. Therefore, PMI is normally calculated by the accumulated degree day/hour model. According to Shiravi *et al.* (2011) the developmental rates in *C. albiceps* and *L. sericata* were highly different in terms of accumulation of degree days required than that of the flesh fly *Sarcophaga sp.* They reported that the speed of development in the flesh fly was slower that blowflies. At 28°C the total developmental time from egg to adult was 13-19 days in *Sarcophaga sp*. While, Jadav and Sathe, 2014 reported that the development was completed within the range of 9 to 11 days in both the species *C. erythrocephala* and *L. sericata*.

According to Hall and Doisy (1993) the amount of time after death affected the structure of the assemblage of insects attracted to a carcass; a feature that will have direct implications on the accuracy of the biological information available to the forensic entomologist. Forest ecosystems are characterized by predator prey relations, parasitism, mutualism, symbiotism, etc. Therefore, forensic insects are supposed to be the indicators of ecologically varying regions and types of forests. The speed of development in the flesh fly was also reported slower than blow flies (Sathe *et al.* 2013). Therefore, temperature requirements of some common forensically important blow and flesh flies (Diptera) under laboratory conditions have been studied by several workers (White *et al.* 1940; Grassberger *et al.* 2003; Shiravi *et al.* 2011). They reported that rates of development decreased step by step as the flies grew from egg to larvae and then to adult stage. However, this rate was bigger for blow flies *C. albiceps* and *L. sericata* in comparison with the fleshy fly *Sarcophaga* sp.

According to Gallagher *et al.* (2010) the development of fly larvae is temperature dependant and in higher temperature, the rate of development increases and duration of development becomes shortened. The variation of developmental times between different populations emphasises on specific characterization of regional developmental times and survival in the region.

The development of blow flies is related with natural and synthetic diet, humidity and competition between larvae (Clark *et al.* 2006). It has been noted that beef liver that are often used in laboratory rearing of flies produce offensive odors and contamination. The presence of toxins in decomposing tissues from natural diets has also been demonstrated affecting the developmental rate of blow flies (Clark *et al.* 2006). On the liver of pigs and cows, the larvae of flies develop very fastly with larger adult size than tissues. An artificial diet, powdered milk caused a lower duration of larval stages in comparison with the animal liver (Tachibana and Numata, 2001). Similarly, overcrowding of larvae also decreased the growth rate of blow flies leading to wrong conclusions (Smith and Wall, 1997). Therefore, biology fecundity, intrinsic rate of increase of blow flies plays an important role in forensic cases. The present work will add great relevance in forensic science and environmental science for wild life protection and conservation.

According to Rivers and Dahlem (2014) carrion-inhabiting insects peak of abundance was during warm summer months, when temperature of a corpse can reach a zenith due to a combination of factors *viz;* solar radiation, tissue decomposition, microbial processes and insect activity. The insect survival was dependant on the ability to overcome or avoid thermal stress. Insect posses a highly efficient general stress response which often functions to produce a series of stress proteins that are believed to confirm protection and repair under a wide range of environmental and artificial insects. Such proteins are referred as heat-shock proteins.

Biogeoclimatic zones experience seasonal change depending on the biogeographic region (Rivers and Dahlem, 2014). Within temperate zones of North American and other regions, predictable climatic change manifested four seasons, with only one, summer, truly conducive to carrion insect activity.

Spring and fall in most areas of the United States displayed reduced calliphorid activity in terms of species diversity and abundance in comparison with warmer summer months. Winter was nearly devoid of all necrophagous insect activity throughout North America north of the Mexican border (Watson and Carlton, 2003, 2005; Sharanowski *et al.* 2008), with the exception of some locations in the southeast (*e.g.*, South Carolina and Florida) and southwest (Arizona and California). Some flies (*e.g.*, *Phormia regina* and *Cynomya cadaverina*) flourish in the cooler conditions of late spring and early fall, but were not adapted for adult activity during hot ambient temperatures of summer and thus entered quiescence, a state of dormancy characterized by reduced metabolic activity but which was quickly terminated with the advent of favorable conditions. Sarcophagids over wintered in a state of pupal diapause.

Another factor influencing seasonal patterns of succession was the availability of carrion. The occurrence of potential food resources diminished during unfavorable seasonal conditions such as: cold weather or rainy seasons. Small vertebrate animals in particular were likely to enter a period of hibernation to avoid exposure to harsh weather. The necrophagous insects synchronize their dormancy with that of vertebrate animals, a feature reminiscent of parasitoid diapauses in step with that of their insect hosts. In fact, the seasonal occurrence of many necrophagous sarcophagids may be aligned with the life-history features of small mammals since it appears these flies prefer small carcasses over large (Denno and Cothran, 1976). Likewise, differences in diapauses strategies between sarcophagids and calliphorids seem to reflect carcass preferences.

Body location after death can have a profound impact on the ability of necrophagous insects to detect, locate and use animal remains. If the corpse is located in a concealed area such as: indoors, in a vehicle, or stuffed into a closed trash can, the chemical cues emanating from the body will likely take longer to escape the concealment to be subsequently detected in the environment than when carrion decomposes exposed in a terrestrial environment. These artificial habitats share similar influences on necrophagous insect activity by functioning as: *(i)* physical barriers to activation/searching and *(ii)* physical deterrents to oviposition/larviposition.

Any location, artificial or natural, that restricts air movement poses a challenge to necrophagous insects in detecting a corpse. The net effect is a lengthening of the exposure phase and a delay in the onset of the activation phase or detection of the body. Foraging behaviour cannot begin until activation, so naturally this aspect of fly activity is set back as well. Factors or conditions that alter activation can be classified as those that: *(i)* delay odor detection and *(ii)* abolish odor detection.

Failure to detect a decomposing body in the environment is rare for any animal, not just insects, which relies on carrion for survival. Competition for the food resource is intense and necrophagous insects, particularly those associated with the first waves of colonization; possess highly acute olfaction finely attuned to the odors emitted from animal remains. Adult flies from the family Phoridae show a remarkable ability to perceive odors of death.

A burnt body may lead to an earlier onset of the activation phase and subsequent acceptance phase, so that oviposition/larviposition occurs sooner than on unburnt cadavers found in the same habitat or location. Burnt tissue is often rejected as a site for egg deposition (Anderson, 2005). Burn damage to human bodies is classified using subjective 5-level scale referred to as the Crow - Glassman Scale. Each level refers to increasing damage to the body that can assessed by visual inspection. Early detection of burnt remains and subsequent oviposition by necrophagous flies is associated with bodies displaying burn damage consistent with CGS level 1-2 (Avila and Goff, 1998).

The attractiveness of such burnt cadavers to Calliphorids is attributed to fluids and gases from the internal environment through cracks and blisters in the skin (Avila and Goff, 1998). Autolysis, putrefaction and algor mortis are temperature-dependent processes associated with body decomposition that subsequently influence insect colonization and development on carrion.

Any conditions that lower ambient temperatures will create the trickle-down effect of slowing the rate of physical and chemical decomposition of carrion. In turn, this decreases liberation of useable nutrients available for consumption by necrophagous insects, which thus negatively impacts growth rate.

Shifts in ambient temperatures near upper or lower thermal limits in terms of the zone of tolerance for growth can retard development. If an individual remains in such conditions for an extended period of time, a halt in development may ensue, leading to chill-coma or heat stupor.

Insect colonization of carrion can vary considerably based on location. A blow fly like: *Chrysomya albiceps* is found in parts of Africa or that *Calliphora vicina* is abundant in Central Europe offers only limited utility in understanding the natural distribution or predictability of colonization for a given species.

Insect fauna are usually referenced with regard to biogeoclimatic zones or terrestrial ecozones. A given biogeographical area is composed of multiple habitats. Surfaces remaining below the water level are suitable for continued aquatic insect utilization. Similarly, shallow bodies of water such as: a creek or stream permit colonization by terrestrial necrophagous insects, while, submerged portions of the corpse can be a resource to aquatic invertebrates.

Some fly species do appear to specialize on colonization of buried bodies and include: some phorids like: *Conicera tibialis* and muscids like: *Muscina stabulans, M. prolapsa* and *Ophyra sp.* (Gunn and Bird, 2011). In general the ecological conditions play important role in life activities of forensic insects and their by showing the characteristics which help in obtaining clues in forensic science. The present work carried out in Kolhapur region will help in forensic science as base line data.

7 SUMMARY AND CONCLUSION

Forensic insects help in solving the problems related to murder, suicide, rape, physical abuse and contraband trafficking. Two major groups of insects that are attracted to carcass and provide valuable information in forensic investigation are the dipterous flies and the Coleopterous beetles. Other insects belonging to orders Hymenoptera, Anapleura, Dactyoptera etc., also play an important role in solving forensic problems. Therefore, studying the diversity, biology, ecology and making the index of forensic insects of a region is essential part of forensic science. The developmental factors of forensic insects tell us the exact time of death of a person. Insects also tell us the route used by culprit in certain forensic cases, the toxicity caused in the case and the environment of forensic events. The carcasses undergoes five stages of decomposition. At each stage of decomposition particular group of insects is associated. In the first stage, especially blowflies and flesh flies are attracted. The adults and maggots of blowflies and flesh flies are most widely used in the investigation. At the latter stages of decomposition beetles dominant the scene. Apart from the use of insects in estimating PMI they have their own economic value. Blowflies and flesh flies cause myiasis in human and livestock.

Therefore, the present topic has been selected for diversity, biology and ecology of forensic insect from Kolhapur district of Maharashtra. Kolhapur is biodiversity rich area under which the famous Western Ghats, 18th Mega biodiversity hotspots of the world is also located in Kolhapur district. Hence the present work has special importance from the view of forensic science.

The book has been divided in to eight chapters. First Chapter is devoted for general introduction which contain characteristics of Kolhapur district importance of the topic at national and international scenario. Second Chapter contains review of literature of the topic.

Third Chapter embodies materials and methods adopted for completion of the work. The forensic insects have been collected with the help of hand picking, swept insect net. Collected specimens have been pinned and preserved in insect boxes. Later they have been described and identified by consulting appropriate literature. Diversity, distribution, biology and ecology have been studied by spot observations at study spots at 15 days interval by one man one hour search method. For morphological (Faunal) diversity of insects, body parts such as: head, thorax, abdomen and their appendages have been taken into account with the help of compound microscope. Biology have been studied under laboratory conditions.

The chapter forth deals with the diversity of forensic insects which includes morphological description of 18 species out of which five were Blow flies namely: *Chrysomya villeneuvi* patton, *Chrysomya chani* kurahashi, *Chrysomya megacephala* fab., *Chrysomya nigripes* Auber., *Chrysomya rufifacies* Macq. while, seven species of flesh flies namely: *Sarcophaga josephi* butcher, *Sarcophaga pes-helicis* senior-white, *Sarcophaga sera* Rohd., *Sarcophaga baranoffi* senior-white, *Sarcophaga pusana* senior-white, *Sarcophaga udhagiriensis* sp. nov., *Sarcophaga orientalis* parker and four species of beetles *Creophilus* sp., *Necrobia rufipes* De geer, *Necrophila rufithorax* Wiedemann, *Saprinus splendens* Paykull have been described. Out of which one new species of the genus Sarcophaga, *Sarcophaga udhagiriensis* sp. nov have been described.

The Chapter fifth is devoted for biology of forensic insects namely: *Sarcophaga sera* Meigen, *Sarcophaga josephi* Buttcher and *Saprinus splendens* Pyk. The above individuals complete their life cycles in 12 days, 13-19 days and 20-25 days respectively. The Chapter sixth dedicated to ecological studies. A total of 27 species of forensic insect have been reported from Kolhapur district out of which 12 species were belonging to the orders Diptera, 4 from Coleoptera, 2 from Hymenoptera and 1 each from Dactyoptera and Anoplura have been found associated with carcasses of dog, cat, rat and buffalo at Kolhapur. Flesh flies appeared very first on all carcasses selected for the present study at a moist stage before 6 hours for egg laying, second arrived insects were blow flies. They occurred before 24 hours and beetles appeared at active stage and the advanced stages of decomposition of carcasses. They were found feeding on the muscles attached to the bones and most interior parts. The maggots of flies were related to feeding on muscles of superficial as well as various organs and interior part of the carcass. The dominant order of insects prevalent in Kolhapur region was Diptera followed by Coleoptera, Hymenoptera, Dactyoptera and Anapleura.

CONCLUSION

Forensic entomology is inexorably a scientific discipline that interprets the information related to death using insect specimens as silent witness in order to provide data not available by using the routine methods of classic pathology. Forensic insects play a very crucial role in solving-problems related to murder, suicide, sexual molestation, child-neglect and abuse. The environment, time of death of a person, road used and unknown place of dead bodies are detected by insects. Forensic insects develop on various vertebrates such as: mammals, birds, reptiles, amphibians, etc. The vertebrate carcasses are good source of food as they contain rich organic matter needed for development for many organisms, including: insects. Insects in nature play a significant role in the decomposition of dead bodies of animals including man. Kolhapur district being diversity rich area, it is very interesting to expose the forensic fauna which may helpful for medico legal practices. In the present work 27 species have been reported out of which one was new to the science. I hope that, the present work will add great relevance to forensic science and will be stimulatory to students, teachers, scientists and environmentalists working in forensic science.

Lastly, the book contains bibliography referred on the topic.

BIBLIOGRAPHY

Aballay, F., H., Arriagada, G., Flores, G.E. and Centeno, N.D. (2013). An Illustrated Key to and Diagnoses of the Species of Histeridae (Coleoptera) Associated with Decaying Carcasses in Argentina. *Zoo Keys* 261: 61-84. *doi*: 10.3897/*zoo keys*. 261.4226.

Algalil, F.M.A. and Zambare, S.P. (2015) Effects of Temperature on the Development of Calliphorid fly of Forensic Importance *chrysomya megacephala* (Fabricius, 1794). *Indian Journal of Applied Research,* 5 (2); 767-769.

Almeida, L.M. and Mise, K.M. (2009). Diagnosis and Key of the Main Families and Species of South American Coleoptera of Forensic Importance. *Revista Brasileira de Entomologia,* 53(2); 227-244.

Anderson, G.S. (2000). Minimum and Maximum Development Rates of some Forensically Important Calliphoridae (Diptera). *J. Forensic Sci.,* 45(4): 824-832.

Anderson, G.S. (2001). Forensic Entomology in British Colombia: Brief History. *J. Entomol Soc. Brit. Columbia,* 98; 127-135.

Anderson, G.S. and Cervenka, V.J. (2002). Insects Associated with the Body; Thir use and Analyses. In Hagland WD, Sorg MH (ed.) Advances Inforensic Taphonomy: Method, Theory and Archaeological Perspectives CRS, Boca Ration, Fla., 173-200.

Anonymous, (2014). "Most Urbanized State". The Times of India. 20 July 2011. Retrieved 24 January 2014.

Anonymous. (2012). Western Ghats as World Heritage site". *The Times of India.* 2 July 2012. Retrieved 24 January 2014.

Anonymous. (2014). "Maharashtra Geography". Government of Maharashtra. Archievd from the Original on 25 June 2014. Retrieved 24 January 2014.

Asenjo, A., Irmler, U., Klimaszewski, J., Herman, L.H. and Chandler, D.S. (2013). A Complete Checklist with New Records and Geographical Distribution of the Rove Beetles (Coleoptera, Staphylinidae) of Brazil. *A Journal of World Systematics, Insect Mundi* 0277; 1-419.

Augaul, R.S. Al-Saffar, H.H. Ali, H.B. and Abdul Rassoul, M.S .(2015). First Record of Hairy Rove Beetle, Creophilus maxillousus (Linnaeus, 1758) (Coleoptera; Staphylinidae) for Iraq. *Int. J. Curr. Microbiol. App. Sci* (2015) 4(4): 82-85.

Azmi, W.A. and Lim, S.P. (2013). Comparative Study of Dipteran Species Diversity and their Succession on Rabbit Carrion in two Different Mangrove Areas of Peninsular Malaysia. *Journal of Insects.*

Bala, M. and Kaur, P. (2014). Insect Faunal Succession on Buried Piece of Pork in the State of Punjab (India): A Preliminary Study. *J Forensic Res* 2014, 5 (6); 1-4.

Barti, M. (2015). *Polleniopsis Annamensis* Kurashashi, (1972). (Diptera: Calliphoriadae) A New Record from India, with a Revised Key to the known Indian Species. *Halters*, 6; 63-65.

Benecke, M. (1855). Infanticide, Momification du cadaver, decouverte du cadaver d'un enfant nouveaunedansunecheminee on if s'etaitmomifie. Determination de l' époque de la naissance par la presence de nymphes et de larves d' insects dans le cadaver et par l' etude de leursmetamorphoses Annals Hyg. Publique Medicine Legale, 4;442-452.

Benecke, M. (2001). A Brief History of Forensic Entomology, *Forensic Sci. Int.*, 120:2-14.

Benecke, M. (2004). Forensic Entomology: Arthropod and Corpses. in. Tsokos M (ed.). Forensic Path Rev Vol II, Humana Press, Totowa (NJ, USA), 207-240.

Benecke, M. (1996). Zurinsektenkundlichen Begutachtung in Faulleichenfallen [Expert insect Identification in Cases of Decomposed Bodies]. Arch Kriminol 198; 99-199.

Benecke, M. (1998). Six Forensic Entomology Cases: Description and Commentary. *J Forensic Sci.,* 43(4):797-805.

Bergeret, M. (1855). Infanticide. Momification naturelle du cadarvre Deccourverte du cadavre d'un enfant nouveau-ne dans une cheminee ou ils'etait momifie. Determination de I'epoque de la naissance par la presence de nymphes et de larves d'Inss dans le cadavre, et par I'etude de leurs metamorphoses (Homicide of a new born child found in achinney and its natural mummification. Determination of postmortem Interval by the use of Insect Larvae and their metamorphosis*). Ann. Hyg. Med. Leg*., 4; 442-452.

Bharti, M. (2009). Some Notes on Medically Important Flies (Diptera: Calliphoriadae) from India. *Halters,* 1 (1); 66-71.

Bharti, M. (2009). Studies on Life Cycles of Forensically Important Flies, *Calliphora vicina and Musca domestica nebulo* at different Temperatures. *J. ent. Res.,* 33(3); 273-275.

Bharti, M. (2011). An Updated Checklist of Blow Flies from India. *Halteres.* 34-37.

Bharti, M. and Kurahashi, H. (2010). *Lucilia calviceps* Bezzi, New Record from India (Diptera: Calliphoriadae) with a Revised Key to Indian Species. *Halteres,* 1 (2); 29-30.

Bharti, M. and Singh, D. (2002). Occurrence of different Larval Stages of Blow Flies (Diptera: Calliphoriadae) on Decaying Rabbit Carcasses. *J. Ent. Res.,* 26(4): 343-350.

Bharti, M. and Singh, D. (2003). Insect Faunal Succession on Decaying Rabbit Carcasses in Punjab, India. *J. Forensic Sci.,* 48(5): 1133-1143.

Bharti, M., Singh D. and Sharma, Y.P. (2007). Effect of Temperature on the Development of Forensically Important Blow Fly, *chrysomya megacephala* (Fab.) (Diptera: Calliphoridae) *Entomon,* 32 (2): 149-151.

Bhawara, H.S. and Singh, S. (2008). Insects Evidence in Legal Investigation. *Indian Journal of Forensic Medicine Toxicology,* 2(2); 9-11.

Bousquet, Y., Bouchard, P., Davies, A.E. and Sikes, D.S.(2013). Checklist of Beetles (Coleoptera) of Canada and Alaska. Second edition. *Zookeys* 360: 1-44. Doi: 10.3897/*zookeys*. 360.4742 ,177 (1) e19-e20.

Braack, L.E.O. (1986). Arthropods Associated with Carcasses in the Northern Kruger National Park. *South African Journal of Wildlife Research,* 16(3); 91-98.

Bunchu, N. (2012). Blow Fly (Diptera: Calliphoridae) in Thailand: Distribution, Morphological Identification and Mediacal Importance Appraisals. *International Journal of Parasitology Research*, 4(1); 57-64.

Bunchu, N., Thaipakdee, C., Vitta, A., Sanit, S., Sukontason, K. and Sukontason, K.L. (2012). Morphology and Developmental Rate of the Blow Fly, *Hemipyrellia ligurriens* (Diptera: Calliphoridae): Forensic Entomology Applications. *Journal of Parasitology Research*, 1-10. *Doi:* 10. 1155/2012/371243.

Burger, J.F. (1965). Studies on the Succession of Saprophagous Diptera on Mmmalian Carcasses in Southern Arizona. M. Sc. Thesis, Uiversity of Arizona, Tuscon.

Carter, D O. and Tibbett, M. (2008). Cadaver Decomposition and Soil; Processes. In M. Tibbett, D.O. Carter. Analysis in Forensic Taphonomy. CRC Press. 29-51. ISBN 1-4200-6991-8.

Carter, D.O., Yellowlees, D. and Tibbett, M. (2007). Cadaver Decomposition in Terrestrial Ecosystems. Naturwissenschaften 94(1):12-24.

Carvalho, L.M.L., Thyssen, P.J., Linhares, A.X. and Palhares, F.A.B. (2000). A Checklist of Arthoropods Associated with Pig Carrion and Human Corpses in Southeastern Brazil. *Mem Inst Oswaldo Cruz, Rio de Janeiro, Vol.* 95(1): 135-138.

Carvalho,C.J.B and Patio, M. (2008). Key to the Adults of the Most Common Forensic Species of Diptera in South America. *Rev Bras Entomol.,* 52(3):390-406.

Carvalho, C.J.B. Pont, A.C., Couri, M.S. and Pamplona, D. (2003). A Catalogue of the Fanniidae (Diptera) of the Neotropical region. *Zootaxa.,* 219:1-32.

Carvalho, L.M.L., Thyssen , P.J., Linhares, A.X. and Palhares F.B. (2000). A Checklist of Arthropods Associated with Carrion and Human Corpses in Southeastern Brazil. MemInst Oswaldo Cruz, 95(1);135-138.

Castner, J.L. (2004). Ultimate Guide to Forensic Entomology: A Review Offorensic Identification Cards, Web-only Essay, URL: http:// folk.uio.no/mostarke/forens ent/review FIFC.html accessed 5 January 2004.

Castro, C.P. Serrano, A., Silva, P.M.D. and Garcia, M. D. (2012). Carrion Flies of Forensic Interest: A Study of Seasonal Community Composition and Succession in Lisbon, Portugal. *Medical and Veterinary Entomology* 26, 417-431 doi: 10.1111/j. 1365-2915. 2012. 01031.

Chehlarov, E. (2004). Revised Checklist of Histeridae (Coleoptera) in the Collection of the National Museum of Natural History, Sofia, Historia *naturalis bulgarica*. 95, 16:95107.

Chen, C.P., Denlinger, D. and Lee, R.E. (1987). Responses of Non-diapausing Flesh Flies (Diptera: Sarachophagidae) to low Rearing Temperature: Developmental Rates, Cold Tolerance and glycerol Concentration. *Ann. Entomol. Soc. Am.,* 80(6); 790-796.

Cruz, A.M. (2006). Crime Scene Intelligence: An Experiment in Forensic Entomology. Washington DC. The National Defense Intelligence College. Occasional Paper 12. NDIC Press. 1-73.

Datta, M. and Parui, P. (1999). Fauna of Meghalaya. Insecta: Diptera. *State Fauna Series,* 4(6): 1-537, *ZSI, Kolkata*. 25: 137-162.

Dear, J.P. (1985). Calliphoridae (Insecta: Diptera). Fauna of New *Zealand, (number)* 8.1-95.

Dekeirsschieter, J., Frederick, CD., Verheggen, F.J., Drugmand, D. and Haubruge, E. (2013). Diversity of Forensic Rove Beetles (Coleoptera, Staphylinidae) Associated with Decaying Pig Carcass in a Forest Biotope. *J. Forensic Sci.,* 58(4). 1032-1040.

Dupont, F.Y.F., Champlain, D.L. Cyrille, A.A.J. and Felix, B.B.C. (2011). A Preliminary Study of Arthropod Associated with Carrion in Yaounde, Cameroon: A First Step in Forensic Entomology in Central Africa. *Journal of Ecology and the Natural Environment,* 3(6), 215-220.

El-kady, E.M., Essa, Y.E.E. and Shalaby, O.A. (1994b). Tropical Interaction of Carrion Attendant Arthropods in a Botanic Garden of Alexandria, Egypt. *J. Egypt Ger Soc. Zool.,* 13 (D) 523-539.

Erzinclioglu, Y., Z. (1985b). Immatures Stages of British *calliphora* and *Cynomya* with a Re-evaluation of the Taxonomic Characters of Larval CalliphoridaeDiptera). *J. Nat. Hist.,* 19:6996.

Erzinclioglu, Y., Z. (2003). *Forensic Entomology. Clin. Med.,* 3(1): 74-76.

Fratczak, K. and Matuszewski, S. (2014). Instar determination in Forensically useful Beetles *Necrodes Littoralis* (Silphidae) and *Creophilus maxillosus* (Staphylinidae). *Forensic Sci. Int.,* 24; 20-26. 32; 376-383.

Frederickx, C., Dekeirsschieter, J., Francois J., Verheggenc, F.J. and Haubruged, E .(2013). The Community of Hymenoptera Parasitizing Necrophagous Diptera in an Urban Biotope. *Jaurnal of Insect Science,* 13(32); 1-14.

Goddard, J. (2007). Physician's Guide to Arthropods of Medical Importance. 5th ed. Boca Raton FL: CRC Press., 24-46.

Goff, M.L., Omori, A., I. and Goodbrod, J., R. (1989). Effect of Cocaine in Tissues on the Development Rate of *Boettcherisca Peregrine* (Diptera: Sarcophagidae). *J. Med. Entomol.,* 26: 91-93.

Goff, M., L. (1991). Comparison of Insect Species Associated with Decomposing Remains Recovered Inside Dwellings and Outdoors on the Island of Oahu, Hawaii, USA. *J. Forensic Sci.,* 36(3): 748-753.

Goff. M.L. (1993). Estmation of Post Mortem Interval Using Arthropod Development and Succession Patterns. *Forensic Science Review,* 5 (2): 82-94.

Goff. M.L., Early, M., Odom, C.B. and Tullis, K. (1986). A Preliminary Checklist of Arthropod Associated With Exposed Carrion In the Hawaiian Islands. Proceedings of Hawaiian Entomological Society, 26: 53-57.

Grassberger, M., Friedrich, E. and Reiter, C. (2003). The Blowfly Chrysomyaalbiceps (Wiedemann) (Diptera: Calliphoridae) as a New Forensic Indicator in Central Europe. *Int J Legal Med.,* 117:75-81.

Greenberg, B. (1985). Forensic Entomology: Case Studies. Bull. *Entomol. Soc. America,* 31:25-28.

Hall, M.J.R. and Wall, R. (1995). Myasis in Humans and Domestic Animals Advparasitol., 35:258-334.

Hanski, I. (1976). Biogeography and Ecology of Carrion Flies in Canary Islands. *Ann Ent. Fenn,* 43, 101-107.

Hanski, I. (1977). Breeding Experiments with Carrion flies (Diptera) in Natural Conditions. Ann. *Ent. Fenn.* 42; 113-121.

Haskell, N., Hall, Cervenka, V. and Clark, M. (1977). On the Body: Insects' Life Stage Presence and their Postmortem Artifacts. In: Haglund WD, Sorg MH; Editors. Forensic Taphonomy: The Postmortem fate of hman remains, CRC Press. 415-445.

Haskell, N.H. (2006). Forensic Entomology. 645-653.

Hayat, R., Richet, R., Bayrak, N. and Pekbey, G. (2008). Contributions to the Knowledge of Flesh Flies (Diptera: Sarcophagidae) from Turkey, with a New Record. Turk J *Zool.,* 32: 385-390.

Holloway, B.A. (1991). Morphological Characters to Identify Adult *Lucillia sericata* (Meigen, 1826) and *L. cuprina* (Wiedemann, 1830) (Wiedemann, 1830) (Diptera: Calliphoridae). *New Zealand Journal of Zoology,* 18; 415-420.

Isiche, J., Hillerton, J.E. and Nowell, F. (1992). Colonization of the Mouse cadaver by Flies in Southern England. *Med. Vet. Entomol.,* 6: 168-170.

Jadav, D.K. and Sathe, T.V. (2014). Altitudinal Diversity of Forensic Blowflies (Diptera : Calliphoridae) of Western Ghats (Maharastra). *Journal of Forensic Research,* 5(6): 1-4.

Jadav, D.K. and Sathe, T.V. (2015b). Diversity of Forensic Blowflies (Diptera: Calliphoridae) From Western Ghats, Maharastra, India. *India Journal of Applied Research*. 5(9): 53-58.

Jadav, D. and Sathe, T.V. (2015). Diversity, Occurrence and Development of Forensic Insects on Dog *Canisdomesticus*L. Cascass from Kolhapur, India. *Int J Pharm Bio Sci,* 6(4):(B) 498-506.

Jairajpuri, S.M. (1991). Animal Resources of India: Protozoa to Mammalia - An Overview, Animal Resources of India. The Director, Zoological Survey of India, Calcutta. Xi-xxvii.

Janaway, R.C., Percival, S.L.and Wilson, A.S. (2009). Decomposition of Human Remains. In Percival, S.L. Microbiology and Aging. Spinger Science+Business. 13-334. ISBN 1-58829-640-7.

Johnston, W. and Villeneuve, G. (1897) On the Medico-Legal Application of Entomology. *Montreal Med. J.,* 26:81-90.

Johnston, W. and Villeneuve, G. (1897). On The Medico-Legal Application of Entomology. *Montreal Medical Journal,* 26:81-90.

Joseph, I.,Mathew, G.D., Sathyan, P. and Vagheese, G. (2011). The use of Insects in Forensic Investgations: An Overview on the Scope of Forensic Entomology. *J Forensic Dent Sci.,* 3(2): 89-91.

Kaczorowska, E. (2006). Blowflies (Diptera: Calliphoridae) in the salinehabitats of the Polish Baltic coast. *Polskie Pismo Entomologiczne* 75 (1): 11-27.

Kashyap, V.K. and Pillay, V.V. (1989a). Insect and Crime Investigations. *What is Forensic Entomology*? I. C. P. R, 12-17.434-7540.

Kashyap, V.K. and Pillay, V.V. (1989b). Efficacy of Entomological Method in Estimation of Postmortem Interval: A Comparative Analysis. *Forensic Sci. Int.,* 40:245-250.

Khoobdel, M., Jonaidi, N. and Rashti M.S.(2008). Blowfly and Flesh Fly (Diptera: Cyclorrhpha) fauna in Tehren, Iran. *Journal of Entomology,* 5(3); 185-192.

Klimaszeski, J., Godin, B., Langor, D., Bourdon, C., Lee, S-I. and Horwood, D. (2015). New Distribution Records for Canadian Aleocharinae (Coleoptera, Staphylinidae), and New Synonymies for *Trichiusa*. *ZooKeys*, 498: 51-91. Doi: 10.3897/*zookeys*. 498.9282.

Knipling, E.F. (1939). A Key for Blowfly Larvae Concerned in Wound and cutaneous myaisis. *Annals Entomological Society of America*, 376-388.

Kosmann, C., Rubens Pinto de Mello, Erica Sevilha Harterreiten-Souza and Jose Roberto Pujol-Luz. (2013). A List of Current Valid Blow Fly Names (Diptera: Calliphoridae) in the Americas South of Mexico with Key to the Brazilian Species. *EntomoBrasilis* 6(1): 74-85.

Kumara, T.K., Disney, R.H.L., Hassan, A.A. Flores, M., Hwa, T.S. Mohamed, Z., CheSalmah, M.R. and Bhupinder, S. (2012). Occurrence of Oriental Lies Associated with Indoor and Outdoor Human Remains in the Tropical Climate of North Malasia. *Journal of Vector Ecology*, 37(1):62-68

Kurahashi, H. (1981). Blow Flies from Fiji, with Descriptions of three New Species of the genus *Onesia* (Diptera: Calliphoridae). *Pacific Insects*, 23 (3-4); 434-444.

Kuria, S.K., Kingu, H.J., Vasaikar, S.D., Mkhize, J.N., Lisa, J.M. and Dhaffala, A. (2010). New Fly Species Causing Human Myiasis Identified in Eastern Cape, South Africa. Scientific Letters, 100(9):580-581.

Lane, R.P. (1975). An Investigation into Blow fly (Dipetera: Calliphoridae) Succession on Corpses. *J. Natu. Hist.*, 9: 581-588.

Leclercq, J. and Leclercq, M. (1948). Donness Bionomiques Pour *Calliphora erythrocephala* (meigen) et cas d' Application a la Medicine legale. Bull. Soc. Entomol. *France*, 53: 101-103.

Leclercq, M. (1969). Entomological Parasitology: The Relations Between Entomology and the Medical Sciences. *Oxford: Pergamon*, p. 159.

Leclercq, M. (1983). Entomologie et Medicine Legale, datation de la mort, Observation Indite. *Rev. Med. Liege.*, 38: 735-738.

Leclercq, M. (1997). On the Entomofauna of a Wild boar's cadaver. Bull. Ann. Soc. *Royale Belge d' Entomol.*, 132 (4): 417-422.

Leclercq, M. (1968). Entomologie en Gerechtelijke Geneeskunde (Entomology and Legal Medicine). *Tijdschr. Geneeskunde.*, 22:1193-1198.

Lord, W., D., Catts, E., P., Scarboro, D.A. and Hadfield, D.B. (1986). The Green Blow Fly, *Lucilia cuprina* (Meigen), as an Indicatior of Human Postmortem Interval: A Case of Homicide from Fort Lewis, Washington. *Bull. Soc. Vector Ecol.*, 11:271-275.

Lord, W.D. (1990). Case Histories of the use of Insects in Investigations. In Catts PE, Haskell NH, eds. Entomology and Death. A Procedural Guide. Joyce's Print Shop. Clemosn. 9-37.

Ma Y. K., Hu, C., Min, J.-X. (2000). A Preliminary Study on the Constitution and Succession of Ins Community on Pig Carcass in Hangzhou district. *Acta entomol. Sin.*, 43(4); 388-393.

Marchenko, M.I. (1980). Classifying of cadaveric Entomofauna. Biology of Flies: The Forensic Medical Role. *Sud-Med.* Ekspert., 23: 17-20.

Marchenko, M. I. (1988). Medico-legal Relevance of Cadaver Entomofauna for the Determination of the Time Since Death. *Acta Med.* Leg. Soc., 38(1); 257-302.

Marchenko, M.I. (2001). Medicolegal Relevance of cadaver Entomofauna for the Determination of Time since Death. *Forensic Sci. Int.*, 120; 89-109.

Market, H. (1925). Die Bedeutung der art der Totung fur die Leichenzerstorungdurch Madenfrass [The Influence of the Circumstances of Deathon the Destruction of Corpses by maggots]. Dtsch Z gesGericht Med (1925), 5; 34-44.

Martinez, E., Duque, P. and Wolff, M. (2007). Succession Pattern of Carrion-Feeding Insects in Paramo, *Colombia, Forensic Sci. Int.*, 166; 182-189.

Mazur, S. (1984). A World Catalog of Histeridae. *Polskie Pismo Entomologiczne.* 54(3-4); 1-379.

Megnin P. (1894). La Faune Des Cadavres: Application De L'entomologie A La Medical Legale. Encyclopele Scientifique des Aide-Memoir Massons Gauthier et Fills, Paris. 1-214.

Megnin, P. (1894). La faune de cadavers. *Application de I' Entomologie ala Medicine Legale.* Encyclopedie Scientifique des Aides. Memire. Masson, Paris: Gauthier-Villars.

Megnin, P.(1887). La Fauna des Tombeaux.C.R. Acad. Sci Paris, 105:948-951.

Modi, J.P. (1999). Modi's Medicail Jurisprudence and Toxicology. 22nd ed. Subrahmanyam BV, ed. Butterworth's, New Delhi. 234-235.

Morales, G.E. and Wolff, M. (2011). Insects Associated with the Composting Process of Solid Urban Waste Separated at the Source Revista Brasileira de Entomologia, 54(4): 645-653.

Morley, C. (1907). Ten Year's Work among Vertebrate Carrion. Entomologist's Momthly Magazine, 43; 45-57.

Nandi, B.C. (2000). Studies on Blow Flies (Diptera: Calliphoriadae) of Sikkim, India. *Rec. zoo. Surv. India,* 98 (4): 1-9.

Nandi, B.C. (2002). Blow Flies (Diptera: Calliphoridae) of West Bengal, India with a Note on their Biodiversity. *Rec. Zool. Surv. India,* 100.

Nandi, B.C. (2004). Checklist of Calliphoridae (Diptera) of India, *Rec. Zool. Surv, India, Occ. Paper* No. 231: 1-47, ZSI, Kolkata.

Nandi, B.C. and Sinha, S.K. (2004). On a Small Collection of Muscid Flies (Diptera: Muscidae) of Sundarbans Biosphere Reserve, India. *Rec. Zool. Surv. India:* 102 (Part 1-2): 11-26.

Nishida, K., Shinonaga, S. and Kano, R. (1986). Growth Tables of Fly Larvae for the Estimation of Postmortem Intervals. *Ochanomizu Med. J.,* 34: 9-24.

Nuorteva, P. (1959a). Studies on the Significance of Flies in the Transmission of Poliomyelitis. III. The Composition of the Blow fly Fauna andthe Activity of the Flies in Relation to the Weather during the Epidemic Season of Poliomyelitis in South Finland. *Ann. Entomol. Fenn.*

Nuorteva, P. (1959b). Studies on the Significance of Flies in the Transmission of Poliomyelitis. IV. The Composition of the Blow Fly Fauna in different Part of Finland during 1958. *Ann. Entomol. Fem.,* 25:137-162.

Nuorteva, P. (1974). Age Determination of a Blood Stain in a Decaying Shirt by Entomological Means. *J. Forensic Sci.,* 3: 83-94.

Nuorteva, P. (1977). Sscrophagous Insects as Forensic Indicators. In Tedeschi CG, Eckert WE, Tedeschi LG, eds. Forensic Medicaine Vol. II. Saunders, Philadelpia, 1072-1095.

Nuorteva, P., Schumann, H., Isokoski, M. And Laiho, K. (1974). Studies on the Possibilities of using Blow Flies (Diptera: Calliphoridae) as Medicolegal Indicators in Finland. Four Cases where Species Identification was Performed from Larvae. *Ann. Entomol. Fenn.,* 40(2): 70-74.

O'Flynn, M. A. (1983). Notes on the Biology of *Chrysomya nigripes* Aubertin, (Diptera: Calliphoridae). *J. Aust. Ent. Soc.* 22; 341-342.

Payna, J. A. (1965). A Summer Carrion Study of Baby pig Sus scrofa Linn.Ecol., 46(5):590-602.

Payne, J, A. King, E. W., Beinhart, G. (1968). Arthropod Succession and Decomposition of Buried Pigs. *Nature,* 219: 1180-1181.

Payne, J.A. (1965). A Summer Carrion Study of Baby Pig *Sus scrofa* Linn. *Ecol.,* 46 (5): 590-602.

Payne, J.A. King, E.W. (1972). Insect Succession and Decomposition of Pig Carcasses in Water. *J. Ga. Entomol. Soc.,* 73: 153-162.

Pessôa, S.B. and F. Lane. (1941). Coleópteros Necrófagos de Interêsse Médico-Legal. Ensaio monográfico sobre a família Scarabaeidae de S. Paulo e regiões visinhas. *Revista do Museu Paulista* 25: 389-504.

Pohjoismäki, J. and Kahanpää, J. (2014). Checklist of the Super Families Oestroidea and Hippoboscoidea of Finland (Insecta, Diptera). In: Kahanpää J, Salmela J (Eds) Checklist of the Diptera of Finland. *ZooKeys,* 441: 383-408. doi: 10.3897/*zookeys*. 441.7252.

Prichard, J.G., Kossoris, P.D., Leibovitch, R.A.,Robertson, L.D. and Lovell, F.W. (1986). Implications of Trombiculid mites Bites: Report of Case and Submission of Evidence in a Murder Trail. *J.Forensic Sci.,*31:301-306.

Queiroz, M.M.D.C. (1986). Temperature Requirements of *Chrysomya albiceps* (Wiedemann, 1819) (Diptera, Calliphoridae) under Laboratory Conditions. *Mem Inst Oswaldo Cruz, Rio de Jeneiro,* 91 (6): 785-788.

Queiroz, M.M.D.C., Mello, R.P.D. and Lima, M. M. (1997). Morphological Aspects of the Larval Instars of *Chrysomya albiceps* (Diptera, Calliphoridae) Reared in the Laboratory. *Mem Inst Oswaldo Cruz, Rio de Janeiro,* 92(2): 187-796.

Ramaraj, P., Selvakumar, C., Ganesh, A. and Janarthanan, S. (2014). Report on the Occurrence of Synanthropic Derived form of *Chrysomya megacephala* (Diptera: Calliphoridae) from Royapuram Fishing Harbor, *Chennai, Tamil Nadu, India Biodiversity Data Journal,* 2; 1-12. *doi:* 10.3897/ BDJ. 2. e1111.

Reed, H.B. (1958). A Study of Dog Carcass Communities in Tennessee, with Special References to the Insects. *Am. MidI. Nat.,* 59: 213-245.

Reed, H.B. (1958). A Study of Dog Carcass Communities in Tennessee, with Special References to the Insects. *Am. Midl. Nat.,* 59:213-245.

Rocha, R.R., Mello-Patiu, C.A., Mello, R.P. and Carvalho, M.M. (2009). New Records of Calyptratae Dipterans (Fanniidae, Muscidae and Sarcophagidae) Associated with the Decomposition of Domestic Pigs in Brazil. Memorias do Instituto Oswaldo Cruz, 104(6): 923-926.

Roe, A. and Higley, L.G. (2015). Development Modeling of *Lucilia sericata* (Diptera: Calliphoridae). *PeerJ* 3:e803; 1-14. *DOI* 10.7717/*peerj*.803.

Rùžička, J. and Schneider, J. (2011). Revision of Palaearctic and Oriental *Necrophila Kirby* and Spence, Part 1: Subjenus Deutosilpha Portevin (Coleoptera: Silphidae). *Zootaxa*, 2987: 1-12.

Rùžička, J. Sipkva, H. and Scheider, J. (2011). Notes on Carrion Beetles (Coleoptera: Silphidae) from India. *Klapalekiana*, 47: 239-245.

Sathe, T.V. (1992). Natural Enemies of some Insect Pests of Economic Importance. *Oikoassay*, 9, 15-17.

Sathe, T.V. (2003). Biodiversity of Braconid Pest Biocontrol Agents from Western Maharashtra. *Bull. Bio. Sci.*, 1, 73-75.

Sathe T.V. (2007). Biodiversity of Wild Silkmoths From Western Maharashtra, India. *Bull. Ind. Acad. Seri.*, 2(1), 21-24.

Sathe T.V. (2008). Mass Production Technique for *Campoletis chlorideae* (Uchida). *Biotechnological Approaches in Entomology*, 3, 64-74.

Sathe T.V. (2009). A Textbook of Forest Entomology. Daya Publishing House, New Delhi. pp. 1-234.

Sathe T.V. (2010). Biocontrol Approaches in Mulberry Pest Management. *Application of Biotechnology in Sericulture*, 21, 229-241.

Sathe T.V. (2010). Biodiversity of Damselflies (Odonata) from Koyna Dam and around area. *Flora and Fauna*, 16, 68-72.

Sathe T.V. (2011). Ecology of Mosquitoes from Kolhapur district, India. *International Journal of Pharma and Biosciences*, 2 (4) (B), 103-111.

Sathe T.V. (2012). Biodiversity of Ichneumonid flies (Hymenoptera: Ichneumonidae) from Western Ghats, Maharashtra. *The Scientific Temper*, 3 (1 and 2), 47-50.

Sathe T.V. (2012). Pests of Ornamental Plants. Daya Publishing House, New Delhi. pp. 1-199.

Sathe, T.V. (2012). Biodiversity of tachinid Flies. (Diptera: Tachinidae) from Western Maharashtra. *International Journal of Plant Protection*, 5, 368-370.

Sathe T.V. (2013). Dragon Flies Production Technology. Daya Publishing House, New Delhi. pp. 1-102.

Sathe T.V. (2014). Ecology, Epidemiology and Control of Sand Flies from Kolhapur Region, India. *International Journal of Pharma and Biological sciences*, 5(4)(B), 1037-1045.

Sathe T.V. (2014). Biodiversity of Cerambycid beetles (Coleoptera: Cerambycidae) from Western Maharashtra. Flora and Fauna, 20(2), 251-256.

Sathe T.V. (2014). Harmful Syntomids (Syntomidae: Lepidoptera) of Agro and Forest Crop Plants from Western Maharashtra, India, *Cibtech. J. Zool.*, 3(3), 22-25.

Sathe T.V. (2014). Recent Trends in Biological Pest Control. Daya Publishing House and Astral International Pvt. Ltd., New Delhi. pp. 1-204.

Sathe T.V. (2015). Insects for Human Diet from Kolhapur Region, India. *International Journal of Pharma and Biological Sciences,* 6(1)(B), 519-527.

Sathe T.V. (2015). Biological Control through Ichneumonids. Daya Publishing House and Astral International Pvt. Ltd., New Delhi. pp. 1-117.

Sathe T.V. (2015). Poisonous Insects of Kolhapur, India and their Treatment. *Biolife,* 3(1), 235-242.

Sathe T.V. and A.S. Desai. (2014). Economical and Distributional Status of Uzi fly *Exorista sorbillans* Wied. (Diptera: Tachinidae) in Sericulture in India. *Indian Journal of Applied Research,* 4(8), 10-13.

Sathe T.V. and Jadhav B.V. (2008). Indian Pest Aphids. Daya Publishing House, New Delhi. pp. 1-211.

Sathe T.V. and Jadav Divya K. (2014). Ecology and Control of Eye Flies *Siphunculina* spp. (Chloropidae: Diptera).*International Journal of Pharma and Biosciences,* 5(4)(B), 214-220.

Sathe T.V. and Mahindra Jagatap. (2012). Taxonomy and Molecular Phylogeny of a New Species of the genus *Anopheles (Cellia)* Theobald (Culicidae: Diptera) from India. *J. Ent. Res*.: 36(1), 71-75.

Sathe T.V. and Jagtap M.B. (2013). Mosquito Diversity and Control. Daya Publishing House and Astral International Private Ltd., New Delhi. pp. 1-281.

Sathe T.V. and Jagtap M.B. (2014). Barcoding in MosquitoesAastral International Pvt. Ltd. pp. 1-90.

Sathe, T.V. and Margaj, G.S. (2001). Cotton Pests and Biocontrol Agents. Daya Publications House, Delhi. pp. 1-147.

Sathe T.V. and R.N. Patil. (2016). Conservation, Protection and Utilization Strategies for Amphibians from Satara District of Maharashtra Including Ghats. *Biolife,* 4(1), 189-194.

Sathe T.V. and Patil S.S. (2015). Chromosomal Diversity in Insects. Astral International Pvt. Ltd. pp. 1-121.

Sathe T.V. and Shinde K.P. (2008). Dragon Flies and Pest Management. Daya Publishing House, New Delhi. pp. 1-179.

Sathe, T.V. Bhoje, P.M. and Desai, A.S. (2014). Floral Host Plants of tachinid Flies (Diptera: Tachinidae) from Kolhapur and Satara districts, India. *Journal of Entomological Research,* 38, 183-188.

Sathe T.V., Inamdar, S.A. and Dawale R.K. (2003). Indian Pest Parasitoids. Daya Publishing House, New Delhi. pp. 1-145.

Sathe T.V., Sathe Asawari T. and M.B. Jagtap. (2011). Mosquito Born Diseases. Mang. Publ. New Delhi. pp. 1-342.

Sathe, T.V. and Jadav, D. (2013). Sarcophagid fauna (Diptera:Sarcophagidae) of Kolhapur district. *J. Adv. Zool.,* 34(2):85-87.

Sathe, T.V. Sathe, Asawari. And Sathe, N.T. (2013). Diversity of Dipterous Forensic Insects from Western Maharastra, India. *Int.J. Pharm. Bio.Sci.,* 4(2):173-179.

Schroeder, H., Klotzbach, H.,Oesterhelweg, L. and puschel, K. (2002). Lader Beetles (Coleoptera, Dermestidae) as an Accelerating Factor for Decomposition of a Human Corpse. *Forensic Sci. Int.,* 127; 231-236.

Service, M.W. (2008). Medical Entomology for Students, 4th ed. United Kingdome: Cambridge University Press; 120-155.

Sharma, R., Garg, R.K. and Gaur, J.R. (2015). Various Methods for the Estimation of the Post Mortem Interval from Calliphoridae: A Review. *Egyptian Journal of Forensic Sciences,* 5; 1-12.

Shayeghi, M., Khoobdel, M. and Abtahi, M. (2011). Encyclopedia of Arthropod-transmitted Infections of Man and Animals. Gashiyeh. 147-150,218-221.

Shin, E. S., Lee H. J., Park, J.H., Ko, K.S., Kim, Y.H., Kim, K.R. and Park, S.H. (2015). The First Survey of Forensically Important Entomofauna Collected from Medicolegal Autopsies in South Korea ioMed Research International,(2015), 1-6. http://dx.doi.org/10.1155/20158/606728.

Simmons, P. (1925). The Ham Beetle, Necrobia Rufipes De Geer. *Journal of Agricultural Research,* 30(9); 845-863.

Singh D., Bala, M. and Wadhawan, B. (2007). Survival of Postfeeding Larvae and Pupae of *Chrysomya megacephala* (Fab.) (Diptera: Calliphoridae) after submergence in Oil. *J. P. A. S.,* 1: 217-220.

Singh, D. and Bharti, M. (2001). Further Observations on the Nocturnal oviposition Behavior of Bow Flies (Diptera: Calliphoridae). *Forensic Sci. Int.,* 120; 124-126.

Singh, D. and Bharti, M. (2001a) Ants (Hymenoptera: Fomicidae) associated with decaying rabbit carcasses. *U. P. J. Zool.,* 21: 93-94.

Singh, D. and Bharti, M. (2001b) Further Observations on the Nocturnal oviposition Behavior of Blow Flies (Diptera: Calliphoridae). *Forensic Sci. Int.,* 120: 124-126.

Singh, D. and Bharti, M. (2008) Some Notes on the Bocturnal Larvipositin by Two Species of Sarcophaga (Diptera: Sarcophagidae). *Forensic Sci. Int.,*

Singh, D. and Bharti, M. (2008). Some Notes on the Nocturnal Larviposition by Two Species of *Sarcophaga* (Diptera: Sarchophagidae). Forensic Sci. Int., 177; e190e20.96; 19-22.

Singh, D. and Sidhu, I.S. (2004). A Checklist of Blow Flies (Diptera: Calliphoridae) from North-West of India. *U. P. J. Zool.,* 24 (1): 63-71.

Singh, D. Greenberg, B. (1994). Survival after Submergence in the Pupae of Five Species of Blow Flies (Diptera: Calliphoridae). *J. Med. Entomol.,* 31: 757-759.

Singh, D., Bharti, M. and Singh, T. (1999). Forensic Entomology in the Indian Perspective. *J. P. A. S.,* 1: 217-220.

Singh, D., Bharti, M. (2000). Forensically Important Blow Flies (Diptera: Calliphoridae) of Punjab (India). *U. P. J. Zool.,* 20(3): 249-251.

Singh, D., Bharti, M. and Kaur, R. (2009). A Simple Method to Determine Age of Pupae of Chrysomya megacephala (Fab.) (Diptera: Calliphoridae). *J. ent. Res.,* 33(1): 65-67.

Smith, K.G. (1986). A Manual of Forensic Entomology The Trusteees of the British Museum (Natuural History) and Cornell University Press, London. 1-205. ISBN 0-565-00990-7.

Sousa, J.R.P., Esposito, M.C. and Filho, F.S.C. (2011) Diversity of Callphoridae and Sarcophagidae (Diptera, Oestroidea) in Continuous Forest and Gaps at different Stages of Regeneration in the Urucu oilfield in western Brazilian Amazonia. *Revista Brasileira de Entomologia,* 55(4): 578-582.

Staerkeby, M. (2004). Ultimate guide to Forensic Entomology: Introduction to Forensic Entomology.

Subramanian, H. and Mohan, K. R. (1980). Biology of Blow Flies *Chrysomya megacephala, Chrysomya rufifacies* and Lucilia *cuprina. Kerela J. Vet. Sci.,* 11: 252-261.

Sukchit, M., Deowanish, S. Butcher, B.A. (2015). Decomposition Stages and Carrion Insect Succession on Dressed Hanging Pig Carcasses in Nan Province, Northern Thailand, *Tropical Natural History* 15(2): 137-153.

Sukontason, K.L., Sribanditmongkol, P., Chaiwong, T., Vogtsberger, R.C., Piangjai, S. and Sukontason, K. (2008). Morphology of Immature Stages of *Hemipyrellia ligurriens* (Wiedemann) (Diptera: Calliphoridae) for use in Forensic Entomology Applications. Parasitol Res, 103; 877-887. *DOI* 10.1007/s00436-008-1072-7.

Sukontason, K., Sukontason, K.L. Piangjai, S, Tippanun,, J., Lertthamnongtham, S., Vogtsberger, R.C. and Olson, J.K. (2003). Scientific Note. Survey of Forensically-relevant fly Species in Chiang Mai, Northern Thailand. *Journal of Vector Ecology*. 135-138.

Sukontason, K., Sukontason, K.L., Piangjai, S., Chaiwong, T., Boonchu, N., Kurahashi, H. and Vogtsberger, R.C. (2003). Larval Ultrastructure of *Parasarcophaga dux* (Thomson) (Diptera: Sarcophagidae). *Micron,* 34; 359-364.

Sukontason, K., Suontason, K.L., Piangjai, S., Narongchai, P., Samai W., Boonchu, N., Sripakdee, D., Ngern-kuna, R. and Siriwattanarungsee, S. (2005). Morophology of Second and Third Instars of Chrysomya villeneuvi Patton (Diptera: Calliphoridae), a Fly Species of Forensic Importance. *Forensic Sci. Int.* 154; 195-199.

Sunders, D.S. Wheeler, I. and Kerr, A. (1991). Survival and Reproduction of Small Blowflies (Calliphora vicina; Diptera: Calliphoridae) Produced in Severely Overcrowded Short day Larval Cultures. *Eur. J. Entomol.*

Szpila, K. and Pape, T. (2013). Morphology of the First Instar Larvae of two Species of *Taxigramma* PERRIS, 1852 (Diptera: Saracophagidae: Miltogramminae). *Polish Journal of Entomology* 82(4): 365-377.

Tantawi, T.I., El-Kady, E.M., Greenberg, B. and ElGhaffar, H.A. (1996). Arthropod Succession on Exposed Rabbit Carrion in Alexandria, Egypt. *J. Med. Entomol.,* 33(4): 566-580.

Tantawi, T.I., Elkady, E.M., Greenberg, B. and ElGhaffar, H.A. (1996). Arthropod Succession on Exposed Rabbit Carrion in Alexandria, Egypt. *J. Med. Entomol.,* 33(4):566-580.

Tomberlin, J.K. and Adler, P.H. (1998). Seasonal Colonization and Decomposition of Rat Carrion in Water and on Land in an Open Field in South Carolina. *J. Med. Entomol.,* 35(5): 704-709.

Turner, B.D. (1987). Forensic Entomology: Insect against Crime. *Sci Prog. Oxf.,* 71: 133-144.

Turner, B.D. (1991). Forensic Entomology. Forensic Science Progress. 129-152.

Tüzün, A., Dabiri, F. and Yüksel, S. (2010). Preliminary Study and Identification of Insects' Species of Forensic Importance in Urmia, Iran. *African Journal of Biotechnology*; 9(24), 3649-3658.

Uiyshen, M.D. and Hanula, J.L. (2004). Diversity and Seasonal Activity of Carrion Beetles (Coleoptera: Silphidae) in Northeastern Georgia. *J. Entomol. Sci.* 39(3); 460-463.

VanLaervohen, S.L. and Anderson, G.S. (1999). Insect Succession on Buried Carrion in Two Biogeoclimatic Zones of British Columbia. *J Forensic Sci.,* 44(1); 32-43.

Varatharajan, R and Sen A.(2000). Role of Entomology in Forensic Sciences. *Current Sci.,* 78: 544-546.

Vass, A.A., Bass, W.M., Wolt, J.D., Foss, J.E. and Ammons, J.T. (1992). Time since death Determinations of Human Cadavers using Soil Solution. *J. Forensic Sci .,* 37(5):1236-1253.

Verma, K. (2013). Forensic Entomology World: A New Study on *Chrysomaya rufifacies* from India. *Journal of Entomology and Zoology Studies.* 1(3); 125-141.

Verma, K. and Paul, R.M.P. (2013). Assessment of Post Mortem Interval, (PMI) from Forensic Entomotoxicological Studies of Larvae and Flies. *Entomology, Ornithology and Herpetology,* 1 (1); 1-4.

WCTMGM. (2014). The State's Forest cover". *Wildlife Conservation Trust, Mumbai.* Government of Maharastra. Retrieved 13 March 2014.

Webb, J.P., Loomies, R.B., Madon, M.B, Bennett, S.G. and Green G.E.(1983). The Chigger Species *Eutrombicula belkini* Gould (Acari:Trombiculidae) as a Forensic Tool in Homicide Investigation in Ventura Country, California. Bull Soc Vect Entomol, 8;141-146.

Yang S-T. Kurahashi H, Shiao S-F (2014). Keys to the Blow Flies of Taiwan, with a Checklist of Recorded Species and the Description of a New Species of *Paradichosia* Senior-White (Diptera, Calliphoridae). *ZooKeys.*

Yovanovitch, G.P. (1888). Entomologie Appliqué a la Medicine Legale. Paris: Librairie Ollier-Henrey.

Zumpt, F. (1965). Myiasis in Man and Amimals in the Old World. A Texbook for Physicians. Veternarians and Zoologists. London: Butterworth and Company; 267.

INDEX

*****